Cooking Kindness

Heroes in the Kitchen

*Our three basic needs are
food, security and love;
they are so entwined that we
cannot think of one
without the other.*

A compilation of Kosher-style recipes

Cooking Kindness, Heroes in the Kitchen,
A collection of recipe favourites.
Copyright Gloria Guttman 2006

This book exists thanks to the dedication of a very special group of people who volunteered their time, efforts and recipes to help make "Cooking Kindness, Heroes in the Kitchen" a reality. We regret any omissions made at the time of printing. Some of the recipes contained in this book may have originated from other sources or in other recipes. We have done our best to ensure all information within this cookbook is accurate. Gloria Guttman and her group of contributors cannot be held liable for any omissions or errors.

Recipes: Gloria Guttman and Contributors
Project Management & Co-ordination: Ellen Watt, Professional Development Resources
Editor and Consultant: Norene Gilletz, Gourmania Inc.
Layout & Design: Lori Abrams Lewis
Cover painting Amistad, Artist Janeth Rodriguez, Willow Gallery
Printing: Bobby & Mark Green, Greenhouse Graphics
Cover Photograph: Jeffrey Dennis
Printed in Canada
ISBN 0-9780205-0-2

Copies of the book can be ordered by contacting:

Gloria Guttman
2300 Yonge St., Box 2444, Toronto, ON, Canada M4P 1E4
Office: 416-440-7999 • Toll Free 1-866-230-3269 • Fax: 416-487-8932
E-Mail: gguttman04@earthlink.net

Library and Archives Canada Cataloguing in Publication
Guttman, Gloria
Cooking kindness : heroes in the kitchen : a collection
of recipe favourites / compiled by Gloria Guttman.
Includes index.
ISBN 0-9780205-0-2
1. Cookery, Jewish. I. Title.
TX724.G88 2006   641.5'676   C2006-900974-0

Dedications

I dedicate this book to:
My parents, who gave me an appetite for life.
My wonderful family, who taught me how to live it.
My husband, for his unending love and support.

I dedicate my recipes to:
Lori and Toba, two indomitable spirits.
In memory of Iliana and Elaine,
who are always in my heart!

Gloria Guttman

Introduction

I was eleven years old when I tried to bake my first birthday cake for my mother. The cake never rose – instead it lay dormant, a failed flat pancake. A thick film of white flour covered our red linoleum floor. My mother having returned earlier than expected, marched into the kitchen and scolded me for having desecrated her "sacred domain". It was then that I vowed to become a better "bulabusta" than mother was.

Throughout my life the kitchen has always been a haven for my emotional self. I can retreat there for hours, and through my cooking, soothe my soul. More often than not you will find me in the kitchen in the wee hours of the night when sleep is no longer an option because food must be prepared for the next day's dinner gathering.

I have a great love of good, wholesome food; preparing it, creating new ways of serving it, and, above all, eating it. After my husband Stanley, and all my family and friends, food may be my greatest passion. Over the past several years I have found another passion – I have ventured beyond my kitchen and found Israel Cancer Research Fund. This remarkable North American organization, with scientists based in Israel, funds cancer research that benefits the world.

Hence, the idea! Why not have a cookbook, full of my recipes and those of other celebrated cooks. These *heroes in the kitchen* have contributed their culinary insights because they love cooking and they love the people they cook for. In short, they offer nourishment for both the body and the soul.

It is an honour and a privilege to dedicate this book to Israel Cancer Research Fund. Your purchase of Cooking Kindness, Heroes in the Kitchen, helps support brilliant Israeli scientists who, themselves, continue to "cook up" and discover new remedies in the fierce battle against cancer.

 # Israel Cancer Research Fund

The mission of Israel Cancer Research Fund (ICRF) is to support Israeli scientists in their efforts to find a cure for cancer.

ICRF is Israel's largest source of private funds for cancer research. Since it's founding in 1975 ICRF has provided in excess of 1500 grants to outstanding researchers in major research institutions across Israel.

The outstanding success is due to the incredible passion of its lay people in the United States, Canada and Israel. Gloria Guttman is a sterling example of a passionate volunteer. She has been a committed volunteer and Board member for ICRF in Toronto, and her passion and advocacy for cancer research transcends to her many friends who reside across the Globe.

It is quite fitting that this cookbook is a compilation of recipes from friends and colleagues whom Gloria treasures, and it represents how her passion, humor and kindness sustains so many different friendships. It is also fitting that Gloria has chosen ICRF as the beneficiary of the profits from the cookbook sales, given her tireless efforts in the hopes of eradicating cancer.

Cooking Kindness is a tribute to both cancer survivors, and to those who fought hard to conquer the disease, but unfortunately did not win the battle. Food is often the source of comfort for all of us and we hope you will also find comfort in knowing that the authors of the recipes have dedicated their unique recipe to a cancer survivor or an unfortunate victim. We salute their courage. Be assured that ICRF is trailblazing towards a cure, and your purchase of this cookbook gets us closer than ever to realizing the mission.

Joy Wagner
Executive Director
ICRF

Sharon London Liss
Co-President
ICRF

Carole Herman Zucker
Co-President
ICRF

2300 Yonge Street, BOX 2444
Toronto, ON M4P 1E4
Tel: 416.487.5246 Fax: 416.487.8932 Email: research@icrfonline.org

Acknowledgments

Preparing such a book is not a one woman job. There are so many people I want to thank and acknowledge. I extend my heart-felt appreciation to the dedicated people who sacrificed their time and talent for this cause:

- Gigi Martinez started the original typing.

- Nancy Posluns did the first proof reading and provided sage advice.

- Maureen Bogoroch-Ditkofsky for her timely, well written contributor letter.

- Joy Wagner, ICRF Executive Director, who inspired the "dedication" idea and for her wise direction.

- Lori Abrams Lewis, my daughter-in law and breast cancer survivor, passionately donated her expertise in creating the cookbook name, graphic design and layout.

- Ellen Watt, Professional Development Resources, my project manager, my untiring friend who has organized recipes, the structure of this book, and me, at my most frenetic times. This book would not have come to fruition without her hard work.

- Bobby, Mark & Rick Green, Jim Robinson of Greenhouse Graphics, who have generously donated their time to ICRF in the printing of this book.

- Norene Gilletz, Cookbook Author and Culinary Consultant, Gourmania Inc., whose expertise cannot be measured in cups or tablespoons, she worked miracles with a very tight deadline.

- Elaine Kaplan, Assistant Editor, assisted Norene with the editing and organizing of the recipes.

- Sharon London Liss, Co-President, ICRF, who was always there to listen and advise.

Acknowledgments

- Janice Jordan, her committee and my friends, who helped organize the selling of Cooking Kindness, Heroes in the Kitchen at the Women of Action luncheon.

- Anne Rogul, Time of Day Calendar Inc., for her invaluable advice and sage consultation.

Additional food kudos go to:

- Shasha Navazesh of Shasha Bread Co. Inc. who has brought knowledge to baking so that all his breads and cookies, be it sourdough, spelt, wholewheat or other grains are delicious as well as healthy.

- Leah Kalish whose purist baking makes for the most exquisite pastries known to the palate.

- James Saunders, Executive Chef of Oakdale Golf and Country Club for reviewing recipes and being as helpful as one could ever imagine.

- Joseph Rovito, Zest For Catering Perfection Inc., for reviewing recipes and contributing to the book.

Most important I would like to thank the tried and true cooks that grace these pages.

Gloria Guttman

Table of Contents

The Cooks, Their Recipes And Dedications

Anita Bender With Anita, only the best ingredients are used, fresh where possible. Her feeling is, do the real thing or do not bother at all. Although she has spent most of her life in the United States, her recipes have a European flavour, since she was born in Germany to a mother who was a fabulous cook. Anita says you must be aware that all ovens are different, pan sizes vary, as do eggs. By the way, she only uses large eggs and for baking only unsalted butter. If you are lucky enough to dine at Anita Bender's, fast that day! - G.G.

Fresh Tomato Tart, German Apple Cake, Noodle Soufflé, Jimmy's Cinnamon-Topped Blueberry Bread and Sabayon Sauce: These recipes are included in memory of my husband Ralph – who loved to eat. Ralph battled five separate cancers over a period of twenty years. He took much pleasure from family, food, sports and his medical profession. Food was always a great comfort to him. These are some of his favourite recipes. - Anita Bender

Geetie Brown Born in Ottawa, married to Herb Brown, they are the pillars of their community, which by the way, is my community too. North Bay, Ontario – gateway to the North. Without them, our synagogue and Jewish life would not have survived there. Geetie is always cooking, baking and entertaining. She has been an example for me, that family, friends and relationships are the most important values of life. - G.G.

Apple or Peach Passion Cake: This recipe is dedicated to the memory of Dr. Anne Balla and her husband Raffi Imre Balla, who graced our lives for five years. This was Anne's favourite recipe which I adapted, substituting the peach passion fruit. - Geetie Brown

Bess' Cottage Cheese Pudding: This recipe is dedicated In memory of Bess Cohen who shared this wonderful "break the fast" favourite. - Geetie Brown

Moon Cookies: This recipe is dedicated in memory of my dear mother-in-law Becky Brown, who lived with Hodgkin's disease for 15 years, despite prognosis at that time. - Geetie Brown

Zucchini Zip Loaves: Recipe is dedicated in memory of our friends Lena and Herb Sparrow. He grew the zucchini in his backyard and she supplied the recipe. – Geetie Brown

Paula Carello Was born and raised in Sault St. Marie, Ontario. She is an aesthetician, and in 1994, married and opened her own business. Still, she makes time to lovingly cook and bake for her family. She says a homemade dinner in her home is a sign of love. Her prowess in the kitchen rivals her talents in decorating and design. - G.G.

Chicken or Vegetarian Cacciatore, Roasted Pepper Rice and Stuffed Pasta Shells: I would like to dedicate my recipes in honour of my late mother-in-law, Suzanna Carello because cooking is a love we both shared. - Paula Carello

Fanny Cava Was born in Italy, to Turkish parents. Both these cultural influences inspired many of the tastes and dishes for which she is so well known. Fanny also lived in Cuba and South America, constantly adding regional nuances to her cooking skills. To be invited to partake in Fanny's cooking is an "epicurean dream come true. - G.G.

Agristada, Borekas and Vitel Tonné: In memory of my niece, Susana Cohen. - Fanny Cava

Myra Cohen My very good friend always disliked cooking, and perhaps even feared it... but after many years of entertaining, she too, has grown to love the art of good food. She has turned out some wonderful recipes here, which she is honoured to contribute. - G.G.

Lemon Meringue Dream, Marinated Broccoli Salad, Marinated Asparagus and Myra's Red Currant Jelly Chicken: I would like to dedicate these recipes to Rosamund Witchel, a survivor of breast cancer. This woman makes anyone around her feel just a little bit better. It's the smile on her beautiful face and the unfailingly kind words she has for everyone. - Myra Cohen

Joanne Smith Cutler Born in Toronto, she wears so many "hats" in her world: sculptor, artist, interior designer and decorator. She is a renaissance woman and a culinary "maven." These recipes that she contributed were taught to me, "umpteen" years ago and have never left my repertoire. G.G.

Crème Brulée, Delicious Rice Pudding and Strawberry or Raspberry Pie: I dedicate these recipes in memory of Jimmy Cutler and my dear mother Lily Donnenfield who appreciated my soul and my soul cooking most. - Joanne Smith Cutler

Phyllis Crystal Phyllis was born in Brooklyn, New York and graduated from Packer Collegiate Institute. She is a voracious reader, a late blooming golfer, tennis player and beautiful knitter (her grandchildren can vouch by their scarves and sweaters). Phyllis gathers her family together almost every weekend to their home in East Hampton and single-handedly creates delicious, delectable meals. - G.G.

Orange Baked Chicken, Pecan Nut Roll and Roast Leg of Lamb with Currant Jelly: These recipes are dedicated to my husband, Fred, a cancer survivor with a positive attitude that is to be applauded. – Phyllis Crystal

Anne Estern I've been to Anne's country home in West Cornwall, CT and I can vouch for her excellent culinary skills. She has worked in television production, interviewing and teaching. She is married to the famous American sculptor Neil Estern. Together they make a formidable pair. Her children and grandchildren live a stone's throw from them and are always in and out of her prolific kitchen. – G.G.

Brownie Torte and Oriental Chicken Salad: These recipes are dedicated to my dear friend Judy Schwartz, who has passed the five-year deadline safely. - Anne Estern

Shaynka Farber The word 'enjoy' describes this dynamic woman. Shaynka is a busy mother and grandmother who has time for everyone. She belongs to many groups, is active in sports and loves her games. She enjoys life to its fullest and this spirit is reflected in her love of baking. We all clamour for Shaynka's "amazing goodies". - G.G.

Blueberry Flan: I dedicate my Blueberry pie to Renee, a survivor who continues to be as bubbly as my blueberry flan. – Shaynka Farber

Chocolate Squares: I dedicate my recipe for Chocolate Squares in memory of my dear friend and mentor, Phyllis who originally gave me the recipe. I'm constantly thinking of her because I'm constantly making them. – Shaynka Farber

Lois Friedman Fine Lois says that her love of cooking stems from her love of eating. Her mother was one of Montreal's finest cooks and hostesses, and like her mother, Lois has a very unspoiled pallet. She does not cook with a lot of herbs and spices because she likes the natural flavour of food to come out. These days, Lois tries very hard to alter her recipes to make them healthier. - G.G.

Chicken on Rice, Toffee Cookies, Grilled Chicken Burgers and Potato Pudding: I would like to dedicate my recipes in memory of my brother, Howard, who lost his battle with cancer." – Lois Friedman Fine

Vera Finkelstein A dynamic lady, originally from Montreal, who brought her energy to Toronto and poured it into community service, especially for Israel Cancer Research Fund. Whatever Vera decides to tackle is done at the highest level. Truly, her "table" is always exquisite. A seven course meal is served at any meeting she holds in her elegant home, accompanied by 14 kinds of candy. - G.G.

Oriental Salmon and Oriental Rice and Wheat Berry Pilaf: I dedicate these recipes in memory of Saul and Esther Glassman, my beloved parents, who both died of cancer. - Vera Finkelstein

Gladys Fogler I have always clamoured after her triple-decker chocolate cake and finally Gladys has given in and contributed it for this book! This cake evokes many loving memories for Gladys. Her aunt made it for her when she was a little girl in pig-tails and then passed the tradition on to her mother Mrs. Farber. Gladys, in turn, bakes this wondrous dark moist cake for every celebration. - G.G.

Three-Layer Chocolate Cake and Chocolate Icing: I dedicate this recipe to Susan Taerk, my best friend, who is a cancer survivor of over 30 years. - Gladys Fogler

Ruth Garbe She and her husband, Albie, are serious about how they raise their children, serious about their golf and equally serious about cooking up delectable storms in the kitchen. Ruth loves creating Friday night dinners and always looks forward to this familial celebration. I consider myself a winner when I am Ruth's golf partner or when I make her mandelbroit. - G.G.

Chinese Chicken: To my husband, Alby, who loves Chinese food. Wishing him continued good health and happiness. - Ruth Garbe

Ruth's Mandelbroit: This mandelbroit recipe is a family favourite. I hope we will continue to have good health and always look forward to enjoying a fresh batch. - Ruth Garbe

Oatmeal Raisin Cookies: I baked these cookies for a friend when she was undergoing treatment for cancer. My friend and her family were warmed by the gesture and comforted by the cookies. - Ruth Garbe

Maria Elena Garcia Maria Elena, originally from Guatemala, makes the best soups in Miami. Her butternut squash soup is one of my favourites. She can't speak English nor can I speak Spanish -- so instead, we speak in the language of the kitchen. - G.G.

Butternut Squash Soup: Dedicated to the women of Key Biscayne, who love my soups, which keep them healthy. - Maria Elena Garcia

Margalit Glazer One of eleven children, Margalit was born in Marrakesh, Morocco and now makes her home in Jerusalem, with my cousin Stephen. Margalit has been a nursery school teacher for 28 years. In her class they not only cook, but also bake fresh Challah every Friday for Shabbat. Stephen and Margalit showed me that a Shabbat dinner was more than a spiritual experience. It lasted from 9:00 p.m. to midnight and consisted of eight different dishes. Everything was made with her own hands the night before, including the Challah! - G.G.

Olive Bread: Dedicated to the memory of my dear father, Avraham Azoulay, z"l, who loved to sit down to a snack of bread and olives and a glass of arak. - Margalit Glazer

Olives And Mushrooms In Tomato Sauce: Dedicated to the memory of my dear father-in-law, Albert Glazer, z"l, for whom this was his favourite dish. - Margalit Glazer

Marinated Basil Chicken: Dedicated to the memory of my dear friend, Judy Hollander, z"l, who did not do much cooking, but who knew how to appreciate the cooking of others. - Margalit Glazer

Marilyn Himmel Born in Brooklyn, New York, Marilyn moved to Miami in 1961 and has been living the "good life" in the sunny South. Her major joys in life are tennis, travel and her love of learning. Her husband and children will attest to her talents in the kitchen. She never fusses, but can quickly pull together a lovely meal with ease and aplomb. - G.G.

Cabbage Salad, Marinade for Meats and Spiced Sugared Nuts: These recipes are dedicated In memory of my dear friend Marilyn Kane who bravely fought cancer for three years. – Marilyn Himmel

Jan Krock Jan hails from Worcester, MA. She loves to cook the same way she plays golf – exacting to a "tee." I have learned from Jan to laugh, not cry, at the game of life. Each meal she cooks is enhanced by the love and joy she brings to it. - G.G.

Andy's Spinach Quiche and Katie's Noodle Casserole: I dedicate these recipes to my dear friend, Tammy Kumin, who loves life and I love her. - Jan Krock

Gloria Lepofsky Gloria is always dishing out loving care through her culinary creations. Glamorous, with flaming red hair, she cooks and bakes exquisitely. Her dinner parties always get a "five-star award." - G.G.

Cranberry White Chocolate Tart: Dedicated to the "sweet-toothed" David Lepofsky, a cancer survivor. - Gloria Lepofsky

Fragrant Chicken and Mushrooms: In memory of my grandfather, Herschel Rosenblatt, who would have approved of this spin on "gedemte" chicken. - Gloria Lepofsky

Onion Beer Confit: Dedicated to Elaine Cooper, a friend and foodie. - Gloria Lepofsky

Pasta with Butternut Squash: In memory of my aunt and best friend, Esther Hacker, who was my cooking and baking mentor. - Gloria Lepofsky

Richard J. Lewis Was born (to me) in Toronto and now makes his home in Santa Monica, California. Richard is a writer, director and producer of television and cinema. He can entertain and cook up a storm "at the drop of a hat." He has a welcoming mat, an open door policy of hospitality, "producing" his own recipes and serving them to his many good friends and family. - G.G.

Pineapple and Raspberries: My great friend, Brett Love, was a poet, an athlete and a culinary artist. Many a dinner party sported his sensational recipes and witty repartee. - Richard J. Lewis

Wabi-Sabi Salmon: To my best friend and the mother of my daughter, Lorl, whose strength and courage in surviving breast cancer is equal to any salmon swimming upstream, against the current. - Richard J. Lewis

Sharon London Liss Sharon is the Co-President of Israel Cancer Research Fund as well as a private art dealer and appraiser. To list all of Sharon's accomplishments would call for an entire page. Her cooking is one of her greatest talents, I have borrowed recipes from Sharon for Passover and her recipes are exemplary and always perfect. By the way, she taught me how to serve tiny baby potatoes, which are delicious! - G.G.

Gefilte Fish: I dedicate this recipe to my great-grandmother, Ethel Budovitch, who instilled her love of cooking throughout five generations! - Sharon London Liss

Gravlax: I smile whenever I read this recipe. My mother, Elca, was one of the most accomplished women I know. Not only was she a well-recognized art dealer, but she was a renowned cook. When she sent this recipe to me, she suggested tins of tomato juice, but thought that apple juice would work just as well! - Sharon London Liss

Spicy Marinated Olives: My dear friend Laurie and I traded this recipe back and forth! Somehow, I always thought they tasted better at her home. She always enjoyed them at mine. I think of Laurie and her zest for life whenever I serve these. - Sharon London Liss

and Tiny Baby Potatoes

Mayta Markson Originally from Winnipeg, Manitoba, Mayta is married to renowned architect Jerome Markson. Mayta has been a studio potter for over forty years, exhibiting nationally and internationally. She is dedicated to her family and has always made one feel so at ease with her kind and gentle personality. Her food truly comes with soul. - G.G.

Black Bean Salad, Chocolate Cookies, Cornish Hens and Mayta's Apple Tart: I dedicate these recipes to my husband, who is my biggest fan. – Mayta Markson

Gigi Martinez Her husband, Angel, and their four children, enjoy a heaven all their own when they are together at the dinner table. Gigi continues the art of fine cooking with traditional dishes from her native Puerto Rico, that she makes with her loving heart and hands. - G.G.

Caribbean Apple Pie and Gigi's Corn Muffins: Dedicated to Martha Velez de Nieves, my dear friend, who twelve years ago confronted the diagnosis and treatment of colon cancer. With her unchanging will to living life fully, her resolve has been to serve those facing the same adversities. Amongst her unrelenting efforts, she has been president of the International Ostomy Association for North America, Central America and East Caribbean, as well as the "Asociacion de Ostomizados de Puerto Rico." Martha is a facilitator for ISCAP (International Stoma Care Advocacy Program), bringing hope, help and education to patients around the world, so they may learn to live their lives to the fullest, as she has done. – Gigi Martinez

Geraldine Morales In 1978, Gerrie came to the United States with two small children to escape the revolution in Nicaragua and found herself in "survival mode." She has triumphed over that difficult time of her life and since then, has become a very successful realtor in Key Biscayne, Florida. She loves her job, her new country and most of all, she loves cooking and baking for family and friends. - G.G.

Geraldine's Lemon Squares: To my sister and best friend, Mary Ellen, whose recovery is sweeter than my Lemon Squares. – Geraldine Morales

Bea Myers Bea is an extremely accomplished woman. She is a retired psychologist and a wonderful writer. Bea is one excellent cook. We play bridge together often and when it is her turn to make lunch, no one ever misses the game. - G.G.

Chicken Oriental, Pepper Steak and Vegetable Chopped Liver: I dedicate these recipes in memory of Esther Myers, cancer patient, beloved by her family and her many students and colleagues throughout North America. - Bea Myers

Annette Naiman A super lady, wife of the late Arnie Naiman, World War II hero. She is always there for those who need her. She expands the meaning of the word "love." A little lady with a big heart for her children, grandchildren family and friends. - G.G.

Annette Naiman's Super-Duper Cranberry Sauce/Chutney: I dedicate this recipe to my family and friends. I have been lucky enough to spend holiday times making this for my family and friends to enjoy. - Annette Naiman

Diane Oille Diane is a dental hygienist who grew up in Northern Ontario. We met in Toronto and we were always in and out of each other's kitchens, swapping recipes and trying them out together on our children. One time, we made my mother's famous Peach Marmalade Jam. After 24 hours in the kitchen, we cemented our friendship forever. G.G.

Artichoke Squares, Chili, Chili Sauce and Date Squares: I dedicate these recipes to my beloved daughter-in-law, Kim. - Diane Oille

Dr. Ricky Pasternak Ricky was born in North Bay. She is a childhood friend of mine, now a practicing clinical psychologist living in Sarnia, Ontario with her husband, Jack. Ricky and I have fond memories of our beginnings and we continue our friendship as our mothers did, sharing recipes, secrets and concern for each other. - G.G.

Chocolate Zucchini Cake, Moroccan Chicken with Couscous and Zucchini Pilaf, Spinach Balls, Vegetarian Lasagna: These recipes are enjoyed by my family and friends. I pass them on in support of the Israel Cancer Research Fund. - Dr. Ricky Pasternak

Nancy Posluns Nancy was born in Buffalo, New York and is a graduate of Cornell University. She is the mother of four children and six grandchildren. She volunteers in the psychology department of Baycrest Hospital, as well as being an active member of Kinnereth Chapter of Hadassah-Wizo, whose entire membership produced the well-known Kinnereth Cookbook. – G.G.

Bran Muffins, Pearl's Melba Toasted Almond Slices: To so many dear friends and family members who have been inspirational in the way they have dealt with this disease – with courage, strength, dignity and grace. – Nancy Posluns

Brooky Robins Brooky, who was born in North Bay, Ontario (along with me) has been my life-long friend. She is an archivist and an engaging woman, interested in all aspects of life. Her love for her family and friends always shines through. Along with Hartley, they gather their flock of children, grandchildren and friends into their welcoming home. Whatever she prepares is lovingly presented. Her fridge is always full, as is her heart. Brooky always says, "The old fashioned way is the way I cook – a little of this and a little of that." - G.G.

Brookys' Cookies, Dijon Chicken Breasts, Janna and Brooky's Brisket and Rack of Lamb: Remembering Pearl Banks for her courage, which was as nourishing as her food. - Brooky Robins

Ronda Roth Diminutive and always busy, Ronda is very productive and accomplished. She crochets and knits magnificent baby attire, and her culinary talent is of the same ilk. I would never hesitate to use any of Ronda's recipes. - G.G.

Green Salad, Filet Roast, Neapolitan and Spanish Tongue: I would like to clarify that the recipes I am submitting are not my own creation, but from various cookbooks I enjoy using. - Ronda Roth

There are two special people to whom I would like to dedicate my recipes. One is my mother, who had a mastectomy 33 years ago. The other is a cousin, who has survived Breast Cancer for five years. - Ronda Roth

Joe Rovito
Joe Rovito was born in Italy and came to Canada at the age of eight. He always enjoyed cooking and assisted his mother, who is a great cook. He started working part time in restaurants in 1978 and by 1982 he knew that this was what he wanted to do. After gaining further experience working in restaurants and catering, he opened Zest Catering in 1999. All I can say is that he is one fine chef and caterer and always saves the day and party magnificently. I have had the pleasure of tasting his ultra cuisine. - G.G.

Veal Tenderloin with Herb Crust: I would like to dedicate my recipe to my uncle, Vince Spagnolo, who enjoyed the family reunions we had and appreciated my cooking. - Joe Rovito

Miriam Rubin
Born and bred in Sudbury, Ontario, home cooking was the norm for Miriam. No restaurants for their family! Miriam loves every aspect of cooking. She continues to read cookbooks and can never pass up a new one. Her heart and soul go into everything she does, especially her succulent baked apples! - G.G.

Baked Apples: This recipe is in honour of my husband, Lou Glait, who has survived two bouts of cancer. Lou loves picking bushels of apples in Collingwood and I use many of them to make my special baked apples. - Miriam Rubin

Miriam's Mandelbroit: This recipe was always a favourite of my late mother's. I enjoy having it in the house, because it reminds me of the many creative ways she varied the basic recipe, such as adding dried cranberries, raisins, macadamia nuts etc. You can even dip one end in melted semi-sweet chocolate. - Miriam Rubin

Sandi Samuels
This honey cake is a specialty of Sandi Samuels' mother, Molly Title. This recipe continues to be passed down through the families of Greta, Sandi and Carole, especially for Rosh Hashanah and other significant celebrations. The original recipe might have been her Aunt Ethel's. Sandy is happy to finally bring it out of the closet and into the community. "I couldn't find a better venue to do so! Shana Tova. Happy baking!" - G.G.

Mother Molly's Secret Honey Cake: Whenever I make this honey cake, I am guided by my mother Molly and my sister Greta. - Sandi Samuels

James Saunders, Chef
From southern England, James completed his culinary training in some of the finest country inns in England and France. Since arriving in Canada 11 years ago, Chef James Saunders has lent his cooking expertise to many prestigious establishments, such as the Sherwood Inn in Muskoka, Waterside Inn in Port Credit, and the illustrious Langdon Hall Country House in Cambridge. His style is described as "modern country house cuisine." Since 2001, he has continued to maintain the highest levels of cuisine as the Chef at Oakdale Golf and Country Club. - G.G.

Cedar Plank Salmon with Grainy Pecan Crust, Oakdale Salad and Oakdale Fish Cakes with Lemon Aioli: Dedicated to my beloved grandfather, Max Saunders. His passion and expertise in the hospitality industry was legendary in England. He was my inspiration and the reason I wanted to succeed in this industry. I miss him and his pastries very much. - James Saunders, Chef

Joni Seligman
Joni enjoys growing, cooking and eating good, tasty food. A life in rural eastern Ontario with her husband Jackie Seaton (also a very capable cook), has allowed for this. Surrounded by interesting people, a mix of vegetarians, macrobiotics and carnivores, Joni is always exchanging recipes with friends and family. Her family, now grown, always appreciated the eclectic menu served each night. - G.G.

Basmati Rice: This is for my Aunty Bobby (Wilson), who enjoyed simple fare despite her preference for dining out. She was a force. - Joni Seligman

Lemony Cranberry Squares:

Szechuan Eggplant: Think of Aden when you prepare this dynamite dish. She is taking on the big C with courage, calm and a warm smile. What an exceptional human being. My daughter is teaching us how to live - Joni Seligman

Rosalie Sharp
Rosalie was born in rented rooms in Toronto's Jewish ghetto. It was there that her mother, passed down the famous "Depression Soup" recipe which you will find in this book. To the disappointment of her parents, who would have preferred either a doctor or an accountant, she married Isadore Sharp. These days, the Sharps jet around the world overseeing the 70 Four Seasons Hotels and checking up on the cuisine that is always superb. - G.G.

Ydessa's Depression Soup, Lemon Turkey and Ydessa's Veal Patties, (Korkletten): This recipe is dedicated to my son Chris, who enjoyed his bubbie's 'korkletten' and was a good cook himself. He made cheesecakes from the late Lillian Kaplan's cookbook. Christopher died of melanoma at age 17 in 1978, before the new research could help him. - Rosalie Sharp

Lisa Slater
Lisa was born in New York City into a family of restauranteurs. A dissertation short of her PhD in medical/nutritional anthropology, she decided that making and serving food was far more interesting than studying about it. Lisa currently works at Whole Foods Market where she opened the bakery there as Team Leader and she is now an Assistant Store Manager. There is nothing she likes better than creating new baked goods and pleasing her family, friends and customers with them. She is the author of "Brownie Points," which is a fabulous cookbook. - G.G.

Chocolate Pots de Crème à la Minute, Crustless Spinach Quiche, Coconut Banana Cake, Steamed Salmon with Salsa Verde and Steamed Beets with Chives, Walnut Oil and Fresh Feta: I would like to dedicate these recipes to Davida Glazer Guttman, a wonderful friend, relative, wife, mother and daughter, whom we think about and miss every day. - Lisa Slater

Pauline Toker
Pauline is an elegant friend who bakes and cooks with such unique flair. Wholesome and delectable food aromas emanate from her kitchen. It is always a treat to be invited to dine with Pauline and Jack. - G.G.

Coleslaw, Crumb Cake and Pauline's Sweet and Sour Meatballs: Dedicated to my late sister, Barbara Goldberg (Halifax), who died at the age of 49. She was a most vital person who was committed to family, community and social causes. - Pauline Toker

Margaret Wayne
Margaret is one of my bridge colleagues who is a marvellous baker. She taught me how to make a very good Pavlova. Everything that comes out of her kitchen is mouth-watering. - G.G.

Pavlova and Pumpkin Chiffon Pie: Dedicated to my mother, Mildred Ginsburg, whose cooking and baking have inspired three generations - Margaret Wayne

Dr. Fay Weisberg
Fay is an obstetrician and gynaecologist in Toronto. She was born in Winnipeg, Manitoba and grew up with her family in Calgary. Fay is the mother of two beautiful daughters, the wife of a fabulous man and the proud daughter of survivors of the Second World War. Fay loves good food and finds time to cater to her family no matter how much doctoring she has to do." - G.G.

Mixed Bean Chilli and Peanut Butter Pie, I would like to dedicate my recipes to my family, whose love and support remind me each day how lucky I am. - Fay Weisberg, MD FRCSC

Toba Weiss Toba is wise and witty, with a talent for writing. Her humour is as good as Erma Bombeck's. She is a very special lady and a great friend of mine. Toba Weiss became the same wonderful cook as her mother, my Auntie Clara. - G.G.

Boeuf Bourguignon, Chicken Chasseur, Fillet Of Some Fish and Nana's Chocolate Roll: I dedicate these recipes in memory of my dad, Dr. Tom Bockner, the best person I ever knew. - Toba Weiss

Nicky Wernick Nicky was born in London, England and came to the USA in 1958, on the very first jet. She has a passion for art and owns a beautiful collection of Pre-Raphaelite art, which is often on exhibition. She keeps busy enjoying her three daughters and all her young grandchildren, yet finds time to travel extensively. Food is another passion of Nicky's. Her salad dressing recipes rival anything you can find on the planet. - G.G.

Fruit Crisp, Salad Dressing and Sweet and Sour Meatballs: Dedicated to the memory of my sporty, handsome, feisty husband, Harold, who died of a melanoma so quickly and unfairly. - Nicky Wernick

Ricky Zabitsky Ricky hails from Montreal and like the Mount, is a "royal" entertainer. She ran a distinctive antique shop (which was by appointment only, so that she could look after you personally). Ricky can be found in the wee hours of the morning, cooking, baking and preparing. The outcome is always tempting to the palate. - G.G.

Honey Basil Chicken, Low Cal Mushroom Soup, White Asparagus with Truffle Vinaigrette: I dedicate these recipes to my loving family. - Ricky Zabitsky

Bernie Zucker First, an 'almost' rabbi, then a prominent ophthalmologist, and now a brilliant cook. Bernie, his wife Carole (Co-President of ICRF), and their numerous children and grandchildren partake in his exquisite feasts. You need to have a roomy appetite to polish off his grand cooking. Bernie's meticulous attention to all that he does in life applies to whatever flows from his kitchen. - G.G.

Baked Chicken and Bernie's Gefilte Fish Recipe: I would like to dedicate these recipes to my beloved nephew Gary Leibtag. He succumbed to cancer at the age of 31 on Oct. 8,1983, when he was just realizing his great talent as a real estate developer. - Bernie Zucker

Helpful Hints

- If your soup is too salty, add a raw sliced potato to it. Bring to a boil for a short time and then remove the potato, which will have absorbed most of the salt.

- To make sour milk for a recipe, just add 2 tablespoons of vinegar to 1 cup milk and stir – voila, sour milk!

- To get more juice from lemons, just heat them quickly (for a minute or two) in hot water before squeezing.

- To separate eggs quickly, break eggs into a funnel. The whites will pass through and the yolks will remain. It is always easier to separate eggs when they are cold.

- Fruit that sticks together can easily be separated if placed in a warm oven for a few minutes (e.g. dates, raisins, prunes or figs).

- Keep bread in the refrigerator during warm weather to prevent it from becoming moldy.

- A piece of fresh bread or wedge of apple in the brown sugar jar will keep the sugar soft, or keep brown sugar in the refrigerator to prevent it from hardening.

- Organic foods are more readily available at affordable prices in most supermarkets. Many people prefer to buy them because they contain fewer pesticides and toxins.

- It is more nutritious to use brown rice and other whole grains instead of white rice.

APPETIZERS

Aïoli

This garlic-flavoured mayonnaise is a
terrific accompaniment for vegetables, fish and meat.

3 egg yolks	**Vegetable Platter:**
4 cloves garlic, crushed	**artichoke hearts, cooked or**
½ teaspoon salt	**canned**
pinch of white pepper	**1 pound green beans, trimmed**
juice of ½ lemon	**2 small zucchini, sliced**
1½ cups olive oil	**4 medium carrots, thinly sliced**
	4 hard-cooked eggs, halved
	black olives, to garnish

In a food processor, combine egg yolks, garlic, salt, pepper and lemon juice. Process until blended.

Slowly drizzle oil through feed tube while machine is running, first by drops, then in a thin stream, until it reaches the consistency of thick mayonnaise. Refrigerate until serving time.

Vegetables should be lightly cooked or steamed, al dente. Arrange vegetables and eggs attractively on a large serving platter. Place aïoli in the center and garnish with black olives.

Yield: 8 servings.

Note: This is also delicious with Chick Pea Salad. (See page 140)

Recipe by C.C.

Artichoke Squares

2 jars (6 ounces/170 grams each) marinated artichoke hearts, drained and chopped
1 onion, chopped
1 clove garlic, minced
4 eggs, lightly beaten
$\frac{1}{4}$ cup bread crumbs
$\frac{1}{4}$ teaspoon salt
$\frac{1}{8}$ teaspoon pepper
$\frac{1}{8}$ teaspoon oregano
$\frac{1}{8}$ teaspoon Tabasco hot sauce
2 cups shredded Cheddar cheese
2 tablespoons chopped fresh parsley

Preheat oven to 325°F. Spray a 9-inch square pan with non-stick spray.

Drain artichokes and save 2 tablespoons of the oil.

In a large skillet, sauté onion and garlic in oil from artichokes until golden. Remove from heat and cool slightly. Add eggs, bread crumbs, seasonings, Tabasco sauce, cheese and parsley; mix well.

Pour into prepared pan. Bake at 325°F for 30 minutes, or until set. Cool before cutting into squares.

Yield: 16 squares.

Recipe by Diane Oille

Borekas

Dough:
1 cup vegetable oil
1 cup lukewarm water

1 teaspoon salt
4 cups all-purpose flour (plus
additional flour as needed)

In a large mixing bowl, blend oil, water and salt. Stir in flour, making a soft dough. Knead well, shape into a ball and let rest 10 minutes. Preheat oven to 375°F.

Take a small piece of dough and roll it out thinly with a rolling pin. Place 1 teaspoon of desired filling in the center, then fold dough over and cut with a glass so that it has the shape of a half-moon. Pinch all around the open edges to seal well. Place on a greased cookie sheet. Repeat with remaining dough and filling. Brush each boreka lightly with egg yolk. Bake at 375°F for 15 minutes, until golden.

Cheese Filling:
1 cup feta cheese
1/4 cup grated cheddar
1/2 cup ricotta cheese
pinch of pepper
1 egg yolk
1 cup cooked, well-drained
  spinach (optional)

Cheese & Eggplant Filling:
1 medium eggplant
3/4 cup feta cheese
1/4 cup ricotta cheese
1 egg yolk
pinch of pepper

Cheese Filling: Combine all ingredients in a bowl and mix well

Cheese & Eggplant Filling: Pierce eggplant with a fork and place on a baking sheet. Bake uncovered at 425°F for 1/2 hour, until tender. Cool slightly; cut in half and scoop out pulp. Sprinkle pulp with salt and let drain to remove excess liquid. Chop well and measure 1 cup. Combine eggplant with feta, ricotta, egg yolk and pepper. Mix well.

Yield: about 4 to 5 dozen, depending on size.   Recipe by Fanny Cava

Grape Tomatoes and Mozzarella Chunks

1 container grape tomatoes
340 grams (12 ounces)
  mozzarella cheese
½ cup chopped fresh basil
1 tablespoon extra-virgin olive
  oil

1 tablespoon balsamic vinegar
pinch of salt
pinch of black pepper

Wash and dry the tomatoes. Cut the mozzarella cheese into 1-inch chunks. Combine tomatoes and cheese with basil in a large bowl. Drizzle with olive oil and balsamic vinegar; season with salt and pepper to taste.

Yield: 6 servings.

Note: Easy, but good and tasty!

Recipe by G.G.

*It seems to me that
our three basic needs are food,
security & love.
They are so mixed and mingled
that we cannot think of one without the
other. So it augers well to cook
and bake with care.*

G.G.

New Potatoes Stuffed with Smoked Salmon

12 baby red-skinned potatoes
1 tablespoon extra-virgin olive
oil
3½ ounces (100 grams)
smoked salmon, finely
chopped
2 tablespoons sour cream
2 teaspoons minced red onion
1 teaspoon drained capers
½ teaspoon prepared white
horseradish
Garnish:
1 ounce thinly sliced smoked
salmon, cut into 24 squares
additional drained capers

Preheat oven to 400°F.

Cut potatoes in half crosswise and place in a bowl. Mix together with olive oil, coating them well. Place potatoes cut-side down on a large baking sheet. Bake at 400°F about 25 minutes, until just tender. Cool completely.

Combine chopped smoked salmon with sour cream, onion, capers and horseradish. Cover and refrigerate until needed.

Cut a thin slice off the bottom of each potato so that potatoes will stand upright. Turn potatoes over and using a melon baller or small spoon, scoop out some of the center of each potato, leaving a thin wall. Spoon about 1 teaspoon filling into each potato. Garnish each potato with a square of smoked salmon and a few capers. Cover and refrigerate. This can be done 2 to 3 hours ahead.

Yield: 24 servings

Tips:
Make these for a large cocktail party.
Potatoes and the salmon mixture can be made 1 day in advance.

Recipe by G.G.

Pesto Mushrooms

12 large white mushrooms	4 tablespoons freshly grated
olive oil for brushing	Parmesan cheese
12 heaping tablespoons pesto	freshly ground pepper
sauce (homemade or store-	
bought)	

Preheat oven to 375°F. Line a baking sheet with parchment paper.

Remove stems from mushrooms. Lightly brush mushroom caps with oil. Place mushrooms, rounded-side down, on prepared baking sheet. Spoon a dollop of pesto into each cap. Top with a sprinkling of Parmesan cheese and pepper to taste.

Bake at 375°F for 8 to 10 minutes. Serve immediately.

Yield: 6 servings (2 mushrooms per person).

Tip: Recipe can be doubled easily. Make these mushrooms using my recipe for pesto sauce. (See page 45 or 63)

Recipe by G.G.

*There is no love sincerer
than the love of food.*

George Bernard Shaw

Roasted Red Pepper and Goat Cheese Stuffed Zucchini Cups

2 zucchinis, about 8 inches long	2 tablespoons pine nuts, toasted
½ cup roasted red bell peppers (in a jar), drained	1 teaspoon minced fresh oregano (or ¼ teaspoon dried)
⅓ cup goat cheese, coarsely crumbled	freshly ground pepper, to taste

Preheat broiler. Lightly oil a shallow tray or baking pan.

Trim and discard ends of zucchini. Cut zucchini crosswise into ½-inch thick slices. Using a melon baller, scoop out most of the center of each slice, leaving a thin shell and base.

Steam zucchini shells. (To microwave them, arrange in a single layer and add 2 tablespoons water. Cover and microwave for about 2 minutes.) Drain upside down on paper towels.

For the stuffing, combine remaining ingredients and mix well; adjust seasonings to taste.

Place zucchini cups in prepared pan. Mound stuffing mixture into each cup.

Broil about 4 inches from top of broiler for about 3 minutes, until the cheese is lightly browned. Serve warm.

Yield: about 16.

Recipe by C.G.

Ruth Rosenwasser's Artichoke Dip

This makes a wonderful appetizer.

1 can (14 ounces/398 ml) whole artichoke hearts, drained
$\frac{1}{2}$ to $\frac{3}{4}$ cup green olives, pitted (with pimentos, if desired)

$\frac{1}{2}$ bunch fresh parsley
1 clove garlic, minced
$\frac{1}{4}$ cup olive oil

Combine all ingredients in a food processor fitted with the Steel Blade. Use quick on/offs, until desired texture is reached. Chill before serving.

Yield: about 2 cups.

Recipe by G.G.

There is no sight on earth more appealing than the sight of a woman making dinner for someone she loves.
Thomas Wolfe

Salmon With Capers

1 can (7¾ ounces/220grams)
  sockeye salmon
3 tablespoons capers, drained
2 teaspoons mayonnaise
1 tablespoon lemon juice
a dab of sour cream
1 green onion, finely chopped

Dijon mustard, to taste
dash of Tabasco sauce (or any
  hot pepper sauce)
salt and pepper, to taste
fresh dill or parsley, finely
  chopped

Drain most of the liquid from the salmon. In a small bowl, mix together salmon, capers, mayonnaise, lemon juice, sour cream, green onion and mustard. Add Tabasco, salt, pepper and dill to taste. Serve with crackers, toast or pitas.

Yield: makes 1 cup.

Tip: Keep the ingredients for this appetizer on hand. It only takes one minute to prepare!

Recipe by G.G.

One of the very nicest things about life is the way we must regularly stop whatever it is we are doing and devote our attention to eating.

Luciano Pavarotti

Spinach Balls

2 packages (10 ounces/300 grams) frozen chopped spinach
1 small onion, finely chopped
2 cups dry stuffing mix
$^1/_2$ cup grated Parmesan cheese
$^1/_4$ teaspoons garlic powder
4 eggs, beaten
$^3/_4$ cup butter, melted (you can use Earth Balance buttery spread)
$^1/_2$ teaspoon dried thyme
salt and pepper, to taste

Cook spinach according to package directions. Drain well, squeezing out excess moisture.

In a large mixing bowl, combine spinach with remaining ingredients. Mix well. Cover and refrigerate mixture for 1 to 2 hours.

Roll into 1-inch balls and place on a lightly greased baking sheet. Bake in a preheated 350°F oven for 15 minutes.

Yield: 14 to 16.

Recipe by Dr. Ricky Pasternak

Sweet and Sour Meatballs

Meat Mixture:
2 pounds (1 kg) lean ground
  beef
2 eggs

½ cup matzo meal
1 medium onion, minced
salt and pepper

Combine ground beef with eggs, matzo meal, onion and seasonings. Mix lightly to blend. Form into small balls, handling as little as possible. Set aside.

Sauce:
½ cup water
1 scant cup sugar
½ cup lemon juice

1 large can (14 ounces/398
  ml) tomato sauce
1 onion, diced

In a large pot, bring water to a boil. Add sugar and lemon juice; blend well. Add tomato sauce and diced onion. Add meatballs. Cover and simmer slowly for one hour. Stir gently once in a while to be sure that the sauce covers all the meatballs.

Yield: 10 to 12 servings as an appetizer.

Recipe by Nicky Wernick

Tofu-Chive

Here is a tasty tofu recipe for your enjoyment.

1 pound (500 grams) tofu	1 tablespoon soy sauce
1/3 cup grapeseed oil	1 garlic clove, minced
1 tablespoon extra-virgin olive oil	1/4 teaspoon black pepper
1 tablespoon vinegar	1/2 cup fresh chives, finely chopped

Combine all ingredients except chives in a food processor fitted with the Steel Blade. Blend until smooth and creamy, about 20 to 25 seconds. Transfer to a bowl and fold in chives. Chill before serving.

Yield: about 2 cups.

Recipe by G.G.

Food is an extension of creativity and love. When we cook for someone in need it is always a heroic deed.

G.G.

Vegetable Chopped Liver

2 to 3 tablespoons oil
3 large onions, diced
¼ teaspoon garlic powder
8 to 10 shelled walnuts (or ½ cup walnut pieces)

3 hard-cooked eggs
1 can baby peas (such as Le Sieur), well-drained
salt and pepper, to taste

Heat oil in a large skillet on medium-high heat. Add onions and sauté until well browned but not burnt. Sprinkle with garlic powder. Set aside to cool.

Process walnuts in the food processor until finely ground, using quick on/off pulses. Add hard-cooked eggs (use whites only, if desired) and process together with walnuts. Add cooled onions and process until finely ground. Add drained peas and process briefly, just until peas are mashed. Add salt and pepper.

Refrigerate before serving to blend flavours. Serve with assorted crackers.

Yield: about 3 cups.

Recipe by Bea Myers

SOUPS, SAUCES AND CONDIMENTS

Broccoli Soup

Oh, so healthy!

6 cups vegetable broth	1 teaspoon lemon juice
1 bunch broccoli	$\frac{1}{4}$ teaspoon finely grated
1 medium potato, peeled and	orange zest
cut into cubes	$\frac{1}{2}$ cup low-fat yogurt
2 garlic cloves, peeled	salt and pepper, to taste

In a large saucepan, bring broth to a boil. Cut broccoli into florets. Trim, peel and chop the stems. Add broccoli, potato and garlic to broth.

Bring to a boil. Reduce heat and simmer slowly, uncovered, for 25 minutes, or until vegetables are very tender. Add lemon juice and zest; simmer 5 minutes longer.

Purée soup in batches in a food processor. Return soup to saucepan and heat through. Whisk in yogurt. Taste and adjust seasonings, adding salt and pepper to taste. Serve immediately.

Yield: 4 servings.

Recipe by G.G.

Cauliflower Zucchini Soup with Yogurt

Yummy!

6 cups water or vegetable broth	1 teaspoon salt
2 onions	1/4 teaspoon pepper
2 stalks celery	dash of cayenne
3 small potatoes	2 heaping tablespoons processed cheese (Cheese Whiz)
1 small cauliflower, broken into florets	2 dabs of yogurt
2 zucchini, grated	2 tablespoons chopped fresh dill, if desired
2 carrots, grated	
4 cloves garlic	

Place water, vegetables, garlic and seasonings in a large pot; bring to a boil. Reduce heat and simmer for 25 minutes.

Puree in batches in a blender. Adjust seasonings to taste. Blend in cheese and yogurt. Sprinkle with dill, if desired.

Yield: 8 servings.

Recipe by G.G.

Diet Soup

1 pound (500 grams) green
beans, ends trimmed
4 zucchini, chopped

a generous handful of parsley
water as needed

Place the green beans, zucchini and parsley in a large pot. Add enough water to just cover the vegetables and bring to a boil. Reduce heat and simmer for approximately 15 minutes, until vegetables are tender.

Let cool, then blend thoroughly. Very delicious!

Yield: 4 to 6 servings.

Recipe by G.G.

Butternut Squash Soup

2 cans (14 ounces/398 ml)
chicken stock or broth
3 tablespoons chopped onion
$^1/_2$ tablespoon chopped fresh
ginger
1 cup chopped celery

$^1/_2$ tablespoon chopped fresh
garlic
1 tablespoon margarine
4 medium butternut squash,
washed, peeled and cut in
chunks

Combine all ingredients except butternut squash in a large pot. Bring to a boil, lower temperature to medium and add butternut squash. Cover and cook slowly for 3 hours. Remove from heat.

When cool, process soup in batches in a food processor until puréed. Return soup to pot and simmer for 10 minutes, stirring occasionally.

Recipe by Maria Elena Garcia

Gazpacho Soup

2 cups diced tomatoes
1 1/4 cups diced green pepper
1 cup diced celery
1/2 cup chopped red onion
1 cup diced cucumber
2 cloves garlic, minced
3 tablespoons chopped parsley
4 cups juice (2 1/2 cups V8 juice and 1 1/2 cups Alymer's tomato juice)
1/4 teaspoon Tabasco hot sauce
1 teaspoon Worcestershire sauce
2 teaspoons salt
1/4 teaspoon pepper
3 tablespoons olive oil
3 tablespoons red wine vinegar
1 teaspoon cinnamon
additional chopped parsley, to garnish

You can chop the vegetables in batches in a food processor or by hand. Place them in a large bowl.

In another bowl, mix V8 juice, tomato juice, Tabasco, Worcestershire sauce, salt, pepper, oil, vinegar and cinnamon. Add to vegetables and mix well.

Chill thoroughly before serving. Garnish with chopped parsley.

Yield: 8 servings.

Recipe by G.G.

Gloria's Aromatic Carrot And Orange Soup

2 tablespoons butter	3 cups chicken broth
1 large onion, chopped	1 cup orange juice (approxi-
4 cloves garlic, minced	mately)
½ teaspoon minced fresh gin-	salt and white pepper, to taste
ger	chopped fresh dill
8 medium carrots, thinly sliced	grated orange zest

Melt butter in a large pot. Add onion, garlic, ginger and carrots. Cook over low heat until soft, about 20 minutes, stirring occasionally.

Add broth and bring to a boil. Reduce heat, cover and simmer until carrots are very tender, about 25 minutes.

Process the soup in batches in a food processor until very smooth, about 1 minute.

Return soup to saucepan and reheat. Adjust the consistency by adding orange juice. Add salt and pepper to taste. Garnish with dill and orange zest.

Yield: 6 servings.

Recipe by G.G.

Gloria's Garlic Soup

Healthy and yummy!

6 to 8 cups low-fat chicken broth	2 potatoes, diced
	celery hearts, diced
2 onions, chopped	2 bay leaves
10 cloves garlic, minced	2 plum tomatoes, diced
2 to 4 carrots, diced	parsley or dill

Combine broth with remaining ingredients in a large pot. Bring to a boil, then reduce heat and simmer slowly for 30 minutes, or until vegetables are tender.

Process soup in batches in a food processor fitted with the Steel Blade. Reheat before serving.

Yield: 6 servings.

Recipe by G.G.

Nothing would be more tiresome than eating and drinking if God had not made them a pleasure as well as a necessity.

Voltaire

Low Cal Mushroom Soup

From the Doral Spa — one of my favourites.

3 white onions, sliced	½ bay leaf
2 tablespoons oil	2 teaspoons lemon juice (to
5 pounds morels and wild	taste)
mushrooms, sliced	pinch thyme
skim milk or vegetable broth	salt and pepper, to taste
for liquid, as needed	3 sprigs parsley, to garnish

(I use a large roasting pan on two burners to cook the mushrooms for this soup in one batch. Otherwise, do it in batches.)

Sauté onions in oil until soft. Add mushrooms and bay leaf. Cook on medium heat until tender, stirring often, about 10 minutes. Remove bay leaf.

Working in batches, process the onions and mushrooms in a blender until puréed. Add skim milk or vegetable broth as needed until you achieve the desired consistency. Add lemon juice, thyme, salt and pepper. Garnish with parsley.

Yield: 12 to 15 servingss.

Recipe by Ricky Zabitsky

Mushroom With Chervil Soup

½ pound (250 grams) mushrooms (preferably cremini)
3¾ cups vegetable broth
⅔ cup light sour cream
juice of ½ a lemon

sea salt and black pepper, to taste
3 tablespoons chopped fresh chervil, to garnish

Wipe mushrooms clean with a damp paper towel. Do not peel; just chop them, stems and all.

Heat broth in a saucepan until boiling. Add chopped mushrooms, reduce heat and simmer for 15 minutes, until mushrooms are soft.

Cool slightly. Purée the soup mixture, then add sour cream and blend until very smooth. Add lemon juice, salt and pepper to taste.

Pour into clean pot and reheat. Garnish with chopped chervil at serving time.

Yield: 4 servings.

Recipe by G.G.

Pea and Asparagus Soup

2¼ cups chicken broth
2¾ cups water
1 large clove of garlic
2 teaspoons Dijon mustard
3 medium potatoes, peeled
 and diced
1 large bunch of asparagus
 (about 24 stalks)

2 cup frozen peas (do not
 defrost)
1 sprig fresh tarragon
¼ teaspoon white pepper
1 tablespoon freshly squeezed
 lemon juice
fresh chopped mint, if desired

In large pot, combine broth, water, garlic, mustard and potatoes. Cover and bring to a boil over high heat. Reduce heat to medium. Simmer covered until potatoes are tender, about 15 minutes.

Meanwhile, in another saucepan, bring salted water to a boil. Cut off tips from asparagus, reserving stalks. Blanch asparagus tips in boiling water for 1 minute. Drain and rinse immediately under cold running water. Set aside to use as a garnish.

Cut reserved asparagus stalks in half. Add to broth along with peas, tarragon and pepper. Cook 10 minutes longer, or until asparagus and potatoes are tender. Stir in lemon juice. Taste and add more tarragon, pepper and/or lemon juice if needed.

Pour mixture into a food processor and pulse until smooth. Return mixture to pot and gently heat (or refrigerate until needed).

At serving time, garnish with blanched asparagus tips and fresh mint, if desired.

Yield. 4 servings.

Tip: If making ahead of time, cover and refrigerate up to 2 days, or freeze up to a month.

Recipe by G.G.

Roasted Squash and Garlic Soup

Adapted from Bonnie Stern's recipe.

1 butternut squash (about 2 pounds/1 kg), halved and peeled
1 tablespoon olive oil or grapeseed oil
1 large onion, peeled and quartered
3 cups (or more) chicken or vegetable broth
2 heads garlic
1 teaspoon salt
1/2 teaspoon pepper
1/2 teaspoon minced fresh thyme (or dried)
1/2 teaspoon minced fresh oregano (or dried)
1/2 teaspoon fresh rosemary (or dried)

Preheat oven to 425°F. Line a baking sheet with parchment paper.

Brush squash lightly with oil; place cut-side down on prepared baking sheet. Brush onion with oil; place on baking sheet. Cut off the top 1/2 from each head of garlic; wrap garlic in foil and place on baking sheet.

Roast squash, onion and garlic at 425°F until tender, about 45 to 60 minutes.

Scoop out squash from shells and place in a large pot or Dutch oven. Cut onion into chunks and add to squash. Add broth, salt, pepper, thyme, oregano and rosemary to pot. Bring to a boil, then reduce heat and simmer for 15 minutes.

Purée in batches in the food processor. If too thick, add additional broth. Taste and adjust seasonings.

Yield: 5 to 6 servings.

Tip: You might want to swirl 1 teaspoon of yogurt or sour cream into each bowl if using vegetable broth.

Recipe by G.G.

Tortellini and Spinach Soup

1 package (10 ounces/300 grams) fresh or frozen chopped spinach
1 teaspoon olive oil
1 medium onion, chopped (about ¾ cup)
2 large cloves garlic, minced
2 cups water
1 can (14 ounces/398 ml) chopped tomatoes (do not drain)

3 ¾ cups vegetable broth (about 30 ounces)
1 teaspoon sugar
1 package (12 ounces/350 grams) cheese tortellini
3 tablespoons shredded Parmesan cheese
¼ teaspoon salt
¼ teaspoon black pepper
1 egg

Microwave spinach on HIGH power for 5 minutes to defrost. Drain well, squeezing out excess moisture. Set aside.

Meanwhile, heat oil in a Dutch oven or soup pot on medium heat. Add onion and garlic; stir and cook for 2 minutes, until onion is tender.

Add water and broth to pot and bring to a boil on high heat. Add drained spinach, tomatoes and sugar; mix well. Add the tortellini and bring the broth back to a boil. Reduce heat to medium and cook for 6 to 8 minutes.

Meanwhile, in a small bowl, mix Parmesan cheese with salt, pepper and egg, whisking it vigorously. When soup has cooked for 6 to 8 minutes, slowly drizzle the egg mixture into the pot, stirring constantly. Stir and cook 2 to 3 minutes longer. Remove from heat and serve immediately.

Yield: 4 servings.

Recipe by G.G.

Ydessa's Depression Soup

"When soup was all there was to eat...can anyone imagine this? Weight loss is guaranteed because it will put you off food!"

In a pot, stir-fry some onions in schmaltz (chicken fat) until golden brown. Remove onions from pot and set aside.

Brown $1/2$ cup of flour in schmaltz, stir-frying it into little balls. Then add the browned onions. Add 4 to 6 cups of boiling water. Simmer for a few minutes. Add salt and pepper to taste.

Yield: 4 servings.

Recipe by Rosalie Sharp

Worries go down better with soup.
Jewish Proverb

Annette Naiman's Super-Duper Cranberry Sauce/Chutney

1 bag (12 ounces/340 grams) fresh or frozen cranberries
1 cup dried mango, thinly sliced
1 cup dried apricots, thinly sliced
1 cup oranges or tangerines, thinly sliced (do not peel)
1 cup fresh or frozen pineapple cubes (not canned)
1 1/2 cups orange juice (fresh or frozen)
1/2 cup crystalized ginger, cut up (optional)
1/2 cup sugar or Splenda

Combine all ingredients in a large saucepan and bring to a boil over high heat. Immediately reduce heat to low and cook uncovered for 5 minutes, until fruit has softened, stirring often. Cool before serving. Delicious served with turkey or chicken. Store any leftovers in the refrigerator.

Yield: approximately 4 cups sauce.

Note: If you wish, you can also add raisins or any other light-coloured dried fruits (but not dates, figs or prunes).

Recipe by Annette Naiman

Cranberry Relish

This is Betsy Weig's recipe.

4 cups fresh or frozen cranberries	¼ teaspoon ground ginger
	1 tablespoon orange zest
1½ cups chopped dried apricots	2½ cups water
	1 cup sugar
1 cup chopped golden raisins	

Combine the cranberries, apricots, raisins, ginger, orange rind and water in a large saucepan; mix well.

Bring to a boil. Reduce heat to medium and simmer uncovered until berries pop open, about 10 minutes, stirring occasionally. Add sugar and mix well. When cool, refrigerate.

Yield: about 4 cups sauce.

Tip: Wonderful with poultry, veal and beef dishes.

Recipe by G.G.

The proper serving of good food sustains us and propels us forward into being the most we can be.

G.G.

Chili Sauce

20 ripe tomatoes, peeled and chopped	1 head celery, chopped
6 peaches, peeled and chopped	4 cups brown sugar, lightly packed
6 pears, peeled and chopped	2 tablespoons salt
6 onions, chopped	4 cups cider vinegar
3 red peppers, chopped	1 cup pickling spices
3 green peppers, chopped	6 bay leaves
	3 teaspoons curry powder

Place chopped fruit and vegetables in a large heavy-bottomed pot. Dissolve brown sugar and salt in vinegar. Tie pickling spices and bay leaves in a cheesecloth bag and add to pot. Stir in curry powder.

Heat mixture to boiling, reduce heat and simmer gently for 2 hours, until thickened, stirring frequently to prevent scorching.

Remove spice bag. Pour sauce into hot sterilized jars and seal.

Yield: 12 to 15 pint jars.

Recipe by Diane Oille

G.G.'s Pesto Sauce

This is a delicious dairy-free pesto.

1 cup fresh basil leaves, chopped
2 cloves garlic, chopped
3 tablespoons roasted pine nuts
$^1/_3$ of a small jar sun-dried tomatoes, drained (reserve half the oil)

$^1/_2$ cup seasoned breadcrumbs (optional)
$^1/_2$ teaspoon dried herbs (your favourite)
1 tablespoon Dijon mustard
1 tablespoon vinegar
$^1/_4$ cup garlic-flavoured olive oil

In a food processor, combine all ingredients except the reserved oil from sun-dried tomatoes. Process until puréed, scraping down sides of bowl as necessary.

With the processor still running, slowly add reserved oil and process until well mixed, about 3 minutes. Adjust seasonings to taste.

Yield: about 1 cup.

Tip: This is excellent tossed with hot fresh pasta. You may want to add some freshly ground pepper. You can spread this mixture on a hot baguette and sprinkle lightly with Parmesan cheese. Place on a baking sheet and broil for 1 to 2 minutes, until golden. Also see recipe for My Best Pesto Sauce (see page 63).

Recipe by G.G.

My Mother's Peach Marmalade

24 peaches
8 large oranges
3 lemons
10 cups sugar

1 small bottle of maraschino
cherries
1 bottle Certo

Soak peaches in boiling water for 5 minutes. Peel peaches and slice in $1/2$-inch slices. Squeeze out the juice from the oranges and lemons, reserving juice.

Process the oranges and lemons in a food processor until finely minced. Combine with peaches and reserved juice in a large pot. Add sugar and mix well.

Bring to a boil. Reduce heat and cook slowly for $1\frac{1}{2}$ hours, stirring occasionally. Watch that the liquid does not complete boil away.

Add cherries and Certo the last 10 minutes of cooking. When mixture comes to a full boil, skim off the foam. Pour into sterilized jars.

Note: For every 2 cups of fruit, stir in $1\frac{1}{2}$ cups (scant) of sugar.

Recipe by G.G.

Onion Beer Confit

This onion relish is excellent with grilled meats and burgers.

¼ cup olive oil
6 cups thinly sliced red onions
⅓ cup red wine vinegar
1 bottle lager beer
⅓ cup brown sugar, packed

1 tablespoon chopped fresh
  thyme or rosemary
salt and freshly ground black
  pepper

Heat oil in a large Dutch oven or heavy-bottomed saucepan over medium-high heat. Add onions and cook, stirring often, for 15 to 20 minutes, until onions are wilted and lightly coloured.

Stir in vinegar and cook until vinegar has almost completely evaporated, stirring constantly.

Stir in beer, brown sugar and thyme; season with salt and a generous amount of black pepper. Bring to a boil. Reduce heat to medium and cook at a gentle boil, stirring occasionally, for 15 to 20 minutes, or until onions are very tender and most of the liquid has reduced and is syrupy.

Let cool, then transfer to a covered container. Refrigerate for up to one month.

Yield: 2 cups.

Note: Try this relish on crostini that has been spread with goat cheese. You can also spoon it onto crostini, sprinkle it with aged Cheddar cheese and broil for 1 to 2 minutes.

Recipe by Gloria Lepofsky

Red Wine and Orange Glaze

¼ cup frozen orange juice concentrate, thawed
¼ cup dry red wine

¼ cup margarine (or Earth Balance buttery spread)

In a small saucepan over medium heat, combine orange juice, wine and margarine. Stir well.

Bring mixture to a boil. Reduce heat and simmer until thickened, about 15 minutes, stirring occasionally.

Yield: ½ cup.

Tip: For use as a glaze for turkey, roast leg of lamb, chicken or fish.

Recipe by G.G.

Hunger is the best sauce in the world.
Cervantes

Orange Cucumber Pickles

2 cups peeled chopped cucumbers	1 cup golden brown sugar, lightly packed
1/4 cup pimento, chopped	1/4 cup cold water
1 cup malt vinegar	1/2 teaspoon mustard seed
2 teaspoons pickling salt	1/2 teaspoon celery seed
1 1/2 oranges	(or to taste)

Combine cucumbers, pimento, vinegar and salt in a large crockery container and let stand at room temperature overnight.

The next morning, drain vegetables, discarding liquid. Remove zest from oranges and grind finely; add to vegetables. Combine all ingredients in a large saucepan. Bring to a boil, reduce heat and boil gently for about 20 minutes, or until desired consistency.

Ladle into hot sterilized jars and seal.

Yield: 4 pints.

Note: This was Grandmother Heffern's wonderful recipe.

Recipe by G.G.

Spicy Marinated Olives

This will keep for weeks - If there are any left!

6 cups assorted black & green olives, drained (preferably Kalamata, sun-dried and/or pimiento-stuffed)	2 tablespoons minced orange peel
	1 tablespoon crushed fennel seeds
1/4 cup extra-virgin olive oil	1/2 teaspoon crushed red pepper flakes
1/4 cup fresh lemon juice	
1/4 cup fresh orange juice	minced fresh garlic, if desired

Combine all ingredients in a large container; mix well. Chill several hours or overnight, stirring occasionally.

Bring olives to room temperature before serving.

Yield: approximately 6 cups. This recipe may be halved.

Recipe by Sharon London Liss

CHEESE, EGGS AND VEGETARIAN MAIN DISHES

Andy's Spinach Quiche

9-inch pie shell
1 cup shredded cheese (Colby, Monterey Jack, Gouda, Havarti or Swiss, lactose-free)
2 tablespoons chopped onion
2 eggs, beaten lightly
1½ cups cooked chopped spinach, well drained
1 cup yogurt
salt and pepper, to taste
Parmesan cheese

Bake pie crust in a preheated 425°F oven for 10 minutes, until golden.

Sprinkle cheese and onion in bottom of pie crust. Mix eggs with spinach and yogurt; season with salt and pepper. Pour spinach mixture into pie crust and sprinkle with Parmesan cheese.

Bake on lowest rack in oven at 425°F for 15 minutes. Reduce heat to 350°F and bake 35 minutes longer, until golden.

Yield: 6 to 8 servings. Leftovers may be frozen.

Recipe by Jan Krock

Crustless Spinach Quiche

½ cup shredded Emmental cheese
½ cup freshly grated Parmesan cheese
2 cups milk
2 cups heavy whipping cream (35%)
4 eggs
pinch nutmeg
½ teaspoon salt
a few grinds of black pepper
1 cup shredded spinach
½ cup sautéed red onions, either in rings or chopped
½ cup sautéed red peppers, thinly sliced
5 fresh basil leaves, rolled and thinly sliced
smoked paprika, to garnish

Grease a 9-inch glass quiche pan with vegetable spray. Sprinkle cheeses over bottom of pan.

Mix together milk, cream and eggs until blended. Add nutmeg, salt and pepper. Add spinach, onions, red peppers and basil. Whisk to blend.

Pour batter over cheeses. Cover tightly with a piece of foil that has been sprayed on one side with vegetable spray. This side should be facing down over the quiche batter.

Place in a steamer. Set to cook. Set timer to 15 minutes. Press start.

When the timer beeps, check to see if the quiche has set. If it is ready, remove from steamer. If it needs additional time, set the timer to 8 minutes and press start.

Remove from the steamer and sprinkle with paprika.

Yield: 6 to 8 servings.

Note: If you don't have a steamer, bake quiche in a preheated 350°F oven for 35 minutes, until golden.

Recipe by Lisa Slater

Fresh Tomato Tart

This is a delicious luncheon dish, especially in the summer when garden tomatoes are available. It can also be served as an appetizer.

Pastry:
1¼ cups all-purpose flour
½ teaspoon salt
1 tablespoon sugar
12 tablespoons cold butter, cut into bits
4 tablespoons ice water

Filling:
½ cup Dijon mustard
1 pound (500 grams) thinly sliced mozzarella cheese
10 medium-sized tomatoes, thinly sliced
1 tablespoon chopped garlic
1 teaspoon dried oregano
1 tablespoon olive oil

Prepare the pastry in a food processor. Combine flour, salt, sugar and butter in processor bowl. Process with several quick on/offs turns to make a crumbly mixture. Slowly drizzle in ice water through feed tube and process just until dough gathers together in a ball. Cover dough and refrigerate for 30 minutes.

Preheat oven to 400°F.

Roll out dough on a lightly floured surface into a circle large enough to fit a 10-inch tart pan. Brush bottom of shell with mustard. Top with mozzarella slices, then sliced tomatoes. Sprinkle with garlic and oregano. Drizzle with olive oil.

Place the tart on a baking sheet. Bake 400°F for 40 minutes, until golden.

Yield: 6 to 8 servings.

Recipe by Anita Bender

A Healthy Green Frittata

2 cups chopped fresh spinach
1/2 cup chopped fresh parsley
1/4 cup chopped fresh basil
4 mushrooms, sliced (optional)
1 1/2 teaspoons grapeseed oil,
   divided use

4 eggs, lightly beaten
1/4 cup water
1/4 teaspoon salt
1/2 cup grated cheese (feta,
   goat, mozzarella or
   Parmesan), divided use

In a 10-inch ovenproof skillet, stir-fry the spinach, parsley, basil and mushrooms in 1 teaspoon of oil until wilted and tender, 3 to 4 minutes. Transfer greens to a bowl and set aside. Rinse skillet and wipe dry.

In a separate bowl, whisk together eggs, water, salt and 1/4 cup of desired cheese.

Add remaining 1/2 teaspoon oil to skillet and heat on medium-high heat. Stir egg/cheese mixture into cooked greens; pour into hot skillet. Sprinkle with remaining cheese.

Reduce heat to medium-low and cook, without stirring, until edges are firm and pulling away from sides of pan, about 5 minutes. The frittata should be mostly cooked, but the top will be slightly undercooked.

Place skillet under a hot broiler for 3 to 5 minutes, or until the top is firm and golden brown. Cut into wedges.

Yield: 4 servings.

Recipe by G.G.

Bess' Cottage Cheese Pudding

This is a family brunch dish and also our synagogue's "breaking-the-fast" request.

Crust:
6 cups crushed cornflakes
½ cup oil (e.g., Crisco)
½ cup brown sugar, lightly packed
½ cup flour

Filling:
1½ pounds (750 grams/3 cups) cottage cheese
4 eggs, beaten
¼ cup white sugar
¾ cup milk
4 tablespoons flour
cinnamon, to taste

Preheat oven to 350°F.

Combine crust ingredients and mix well. Reserve ½ cup crumb mixture for topping. Pat the remainder into a greased 9-inch x 13-inch baking pan.

Combine filling ingredients, mix well and pour onto crust. Sprinkle with reserved crumb mixture. Bake at 350°F for 45 minutes, until golden. Excellent served warm, topped with sour cream or fruit yogurt.

Yield: 12 servings.

Recipe by Geetie Brown

Donna's Cheese Entrée

10 to 12 slices challah, cut ½-inch thick	¼ teaspoon paprika
10 slices Monterey Jack cheese, thinly sliced	½ teaspoon salt
	½ teaspoon onion powder
10 slices Colby cheese	¼ teaspoon white pepper
8 large eggs, lightly beaten	¼ teaspoon cayenne
4 cups milk	1 teaspoon Worcestershire sauce
1 teaspoon brown sugar	1 teaspoon dry mustard

Grease a 9-inch x 13-inch glass casserole. Remove crusts from bread; lightly butter each slice.

Place a layer of bread slices in the bottom of prepared casserole. Top with a layer of Monterey Jack, then another layer of bread, ending with Colby cheese.

Combine eggs, milk and seasonings in a large bowl and blend well. Pour evenly over top of casserole. Cover and refrigerate for 8 to 24 hours.

Bring to room temperature before baking. Preheat oven to 325°F. Bake until puffed and golden, about 50 to 60 minutes.

Yield: 8 to 10 servings.

Tips: Skim milk or lactaid milk may be substituted. This tastes best when assembled a day in advance, refrigerated overnight, then baked just before serving. You need to bake this first if you want to freeze it. Wrap well and freeze. When needed, defrost overnight in the refrigerator; then reheat. It's almost as good!

Recipe by G.G.

Katie's Noodle Casserole

1 package (12 ounces/340 grams) egg noodles
1 cup (½ pound) butter, melted
1 cup sour cream
4 eggs, lightly beaten
½ cup sugar

1 teaspoon vanilla
1 can (16 ounces/454 grams) crushed pineapple, drained
cornflake crumbs
cinnamon

Preheat oven to 325°F. Butter a 9-inch x 13-inch glass casserole.

Cook noodles in boiling salted water according to package instructions; drain well.

In a large bowl, mix together melted butter, sour cream, eggs, sugar, vanilla and drained pineapple. Mix with noodles and pour into prepared casserole. Top with cornflake crumbs and cinnamon. Bake at 325°F for 1 hour, or until golden.

Yield: 8 to 10 servings. Reheats well.

Recipe by Jan Krock

The more you eat, the less flavour; the less you eat, the more flavour.
Chinese Proverb

Lois' Noodle Pudding

1 package (12 ounces/340 grams) very thin noodles
½ cup (¼ pound) butter or Earth Balance buttery spread

4 eggs, well beaten
1 teaspoon sugar
salt and pepper, to taste

Preheat oven to 375°F.

Cook noodles according to package directions; drain well.

Melt butter in a Pyrex 9-inch x 13-inch Pyrex baking dish and swish around in dish to coat well.

Combine noodles with melted butter. Add eggs, sugar, salt and pepper; mix well. Pour into baking dish.

Bake at 375°F for 45 minutes, or until golden brown.

Yield: 12 servings.

Tip: You may freeze this pudding. Thaw, then cut it into squares and reheat.

Recipe by G.G.

Noodle Soufflé

1 package (8 ounces/250 grams) noodles
6 eggs, beaten
½ cup sugar
1 teaspoon vanilla
1 pound (500 grams/2 cups) cottage cheese
1 cup sour cream
1 pound (500 grams/2 cups) farmer's cheese
¼ pound (125 grams/½ cup) cream cheese
1½ cups milk

Preheat oven to 350°F. Grease a 9-inch x 13-inch glass casserole.

Cook noodles in boiling salted water according to package directions; drain well.

In a large bowl, mix together eggs, sugar, vanilla and sour cream. Add cottage cheese, farmer's cheese, cream cheese and milk; blend well.

Stir in cooked noodles and pour into prepared casserole. Bake at 350°F for 1 hour, or until golden.

Yield: 8 to 10 servings.

Notes: Sometimes I top this with crushed cornflakes and sprinkle with cinnamon and sugar. This is best served hot shortly after coming out of the oven, but it also freezes and reheats well. For a noodle kugel, this is very light.

Recipe by Anita Bender

Pasta with Butternut Squash

2 medium butternut squash, peeled, cut into ½-inch cubes
1 pound (500 grams) bow tie pasta
4 teaspoons melted butter
½ cup low-sodium vegetable broth
2 tablespoons chopped fresh sage or thyme
2 teaspoons salt
½ teaspoon freshly ground pepper

2 tablespoons freshly grated Parmesan cheese

Topping:
½ cup bread crumbs
2 teaspoons chopped fresh sage or thyme
½ teaspoon salt
½ teaspoon pepper
1 tablespoon grated Parmesan cheese

Preheat the oven to 375°F. Spread out squash in a single layer on a greased baking sheet. Roast until tender, about 25 minutes, stirring once or twice.

Bring a large pot of salted water to a boil. Add the pasta and cook until al dente, about 11 minutes. Drain, rinse and drain again.

Reduce oven temperature to 350°F. Place pasta back in the pot; add squash, butter, broth, sage, salt, pepper and Parmesan cheese. Toss to mix well. Place in a greased ovenproof casserole.

Topping: In a small bowl, combine bread crumbs, sage, salt, pepper and Parmesan cheese; mix well. Sprinkle mixture over top of pasta.

Bake at 375°F for 15 minutes, until golden. Serve immediately.

Yield: 4 servings.

Recipe by Gloria Lepofsky

Pasta with Pesto

1 potato, peeled and diced	1 cup homemade or commer-
1 pound (500 grams) pasta	cial pesto (see My Best
1 bunch broccoli, trimmed and	Pesto Sauce, next page)
cut into 1-inch pieces	2 tablespoons butter or garlic-
1 cup liquid from the cooked	flavoured olive oil
pasta	1 teaspoon salt, to taste

Bring a large pot of water to boil. Add salt.

Add potato and cook 5 minutes. Add pasta and cook 5 minutes longer. Add broccoli and cook 6 to 7 minutes more, until pasta is al dente.

Drain pasta, reserving 1 cup of the cooking liquid. Place drained pasta, potatoes and broccoli in the empty pasta pot on low heat. Add reserved cooking liquid, pesto, butter and salt; toss well for 1 to 2 minutes. Taste and adjust seasonings to your liking.

Yield: 6 to 7 servings.

Recipe by G.G.

One of the secrets of a happy life is continuous small treats.

Iris Murdoch

My Best Pesto Sauce

There's nothing better than fresh basil from my sister's garden!

2 cups fresh basil leaves,
   tightly packed
1 cup fresh parsley or spinach
2 cloves garlic
¼ cup pine nuts, lightly toasted

½ cup grated Parmesan
   cheese (see Notes below)
1 teaspoon or more salt
¼ cup olive oil

Combine all ingredients in a food processor and process until blended, about 15 to 20 seconds.

Yield: about 2½ cups.

Notes: Also see my recipe for G.G.'s Pesto Sauce, which is dairy-free. (See Index for page number.) If any of your guests are lactose-intolerant, omit Parmesan cheese from pesto sauce and sprinkle it on at serving time for those who can have it.

Recipe by G.G.

Eat little, sleep sound.
Iranian Proverb

Stuffed Pasta Shells

This is a quick and easy way to get the taste of my mom's homemade ravioli without most of the work!

1 box (1 pound/500 grams) jumbo pasta shells	2 eggs
	$\frac{1}{2}$ cup chopped fresh parsley
1 package (10 ounces/300 grams) frozen chopped spinach	salt and freshly ground black pepper, to taste
	2 cups homemade tomato sauce (or store-bought)
3$\frac{1}{2}$ cups low-fat ricotta cheese	
$\frac{1}{2}$ cup grated Romano cheese (approximately)	$\frac{1}{2}$ cup grated mozzarella cheese

Cook pasta shells in boiling salted water according to package directions; drain well. Thaw spinach; squeeze it between paper towels to remove excess water.

Preheat oven to 350°F. Grease a 9-inch x 13-inch glass casserole.

In a large bowl, combine spinach, ricotta cheese, eggs, Romano cheese, parsley, salt and pepper. Mix well.

Pour 1$\frac{1}{2}$ cups of tomato sauce into bottom of prepared casserole. Pick up a shell in one hand. Using a tablespoon, scoop the cheese filling into the shell, filling it generously. Place the filled shell in the casserole. Continue until you have used up the filling. You may have some shells left over.

Spoon a bit of the remaining sauce over each shell; sprinkle with grated mozzarella (or more Romano cheese).

Bake at 350°F for 15 minutes, until cheese is melted and sauce is bubbly. (Or wrap it tightly and freeze unbaked for a future meal.)

Yield: 6 servings.

Recipe by Paula Carello

Tubetti Pasta in Diced Tomato and Avocado Sauce

Quick and great!

2 cloves garlic, minced	1 lemon, divided use
1/2 cup extra-virgin olive oil or grapeseed oil, divided use	salt and pepper to taste
3 large ripe tomatoes, chopped	1 pound (500 grams) imported dried tubetti pasta
12 large chopped fresh basil leaves	1 large avocado
	capers, if desired

In a small skillet, sauté garlic in 1 teaspoon of the oil on medium heat for 1 minute.

Combine garlic, tomatoes and basil in a small bowl. Add remaining olive oil and the juice of 1/2 lemon. Season with salt and pepper and let marinate for at least 1 hour.

Cook pasta according to package directions. While pasta is cooking, peel, pit and dice the avocado. Place it in a small bowl and season with salt and remaining lemon juice.

When pasta is al dente, drain well. Place pasta in a serving bowl; toss with tomato mixture. Gently spoon avocado and lemon juice over pasta. Sprinkle with capers.

Yield: 4 to 6 servings.

Recipe by G.G.

Vegetarian Lasagna

6 to 8 lasagna noodles
$\frac{1}{2}$ cup chopped onion
$\frac{1}{4}$ cup chopped celery
1 clove garlic, crushed (or $\frac{1}{2}$
  teaspoon garlic powder)
2 tablespoons vegetable oil
1$\frac{1}{2}$ cups mushrooms, sliced
1 can (14 ounces/398 ml)
  tomato sauce
1 can (5$\frac{1}{2}$ ounces/156 ml)
  tomato paste
1 teaspoon salt
1 teaspoon sugar
$\frac{1}{2}$ teaspoon rock pepper
  (a blend of pepper and
  seasonings)

$\frac{1}{2}$ teaspoon dried oregano
$\frac{1}{2}$ teaspoon each dried thyme
  and dried basil
$\frac{1}{2}$ pound (250 grams/1 cup)
  ricotta cheese or dry cottage
  cheese
1 egg
2 tablespoons chopped fresh
  parsley
$\frac{1}{2}$ teaspoon salt
2 cups chopped cooked
  spinach, well-drained
8 ounces (250 grams)
  mozzarella cheese, sliced
$\frac{1}{4}$ cup grated Parmesan
  cheese

Preheat oven to 350°F. Grease a 9-inch x 13-inch glass casserole.

Cook noodles in boiling salted water according to package directions; drain well. Lay out flat on a towel. Meanwhile, prepare sauce: In a large skillet, cook onion, celery and garlic in oil until soft, 6 to 8 minutes. Add mushrooms and cook 2 to 3 minutes longer. Stir in tomato sauce, tomato paste and seasonings. Simmer uncovered for 10 minutes.

Mix ricotta cheese with egg, parsley and $\frac{1}{2}$ teaspoon salt.

To assemble: Spread $\frac{1}{2}$ cup of sauce mixture in prepared casserole. Arrange half the cooked noodles over sauce. Spread half the ricotta mixture onto noodles, then half the spinach. Add half of the remaining tomato sauce, then half the mozzarella. Repeat from the noodle layer (noodles, ricotta mixture, spinach, sauce and mozzarella). Sprinkle with Parmesan cheese. Bake at 350°F for 30 to 40 minutes. Let stand a few minutes before cutting.

Yield: 6 to 8 servings.

Recipe by Dr. Ricky Pasternak

Vegetable Wraps

⅓ cup light mayonnaise	1 tomato, chopped
1 to 2 teaspoons Dijon mustard	1½ cups alfalfa sprouts
6 large Casa Mendoza tortillas	1 avocado, peeled, pitted and
(or any thin tortillas)	thinly sliced
1 English cucumber, trimmed	1½ cups mozzarella (lactose)
and thinly sliced	yogurt cheese, shredded
1 small red onion, thinly sliced	

Mix mayonnaise with mustard. Lightly spread each tortilla with mayonnaise mixture, leaving a ½-inch border around outside edge of each tortilla so it will stick together when rolled up.

Place a narrow row of cucumber slices along bottom edge of each tortilla. Add a row of onion, then tomato, then alfalfa sprouts, then avocado; end with cheese. Roll each tortilla up tightly. (Roll up partway, starting from the bottom edge to enclose filling. Fold in both sides; then finish rolling up.) Serve immediately.

Yield: 6 servings.

Recipe by G.G.

One cannot think well, love well,
sleep well if one has not dined well.
Virginia Wolfe

Mixed Bean Chili (Vegetarian)

1 tablespoon vegetable oil
2 onions, chopped
4 cloves garlic, chopped
3 tablespoons chili powder
1 teaspoon cumin
1 teaspoon paprika
1 teaspoon oregano
salt to taste
$\frac{1}{2}$ teaspoon pepper

1 can (28 ounces/796 ml)
plum tomatoes
4 cups assorted canned beans,
rinsed and drained
3 jalapeno peppers, seeded
and diced
2 tablespoons chopped fresh
parsley, to garnish

Heat oil in a large, heavy-bottomed pot on medium heat. Add onions and garlic and cook until softened, about 5 minutes. Add chili powder, cumin, paprika, oregano, salt and pepper. Stir in tomatoes, drained beans and jalapeno peppers.

Bring mixture to a boil. Reduce heat, cover and simmer slowly for 1 to 2 hours, stirring occasionally. The longer you cook it, the better it tastes. Garnish with chopped parsley.

Yield: 6 servings.

Recipe by Dr. Fay Weisberg

FISH

Bernie's Gefilte Fish Recipe

Stock:	assorted fresh herbs (thyme and parsley)
2 pounds (1 kg) fish bones and heads from white-fleshed fish	Fish:
4 carrots, sliced	1½ large carrots
2 medium onions, sliced	3 lbs ground fish, divided use
3 tablespoons sugar	¼ to ½ cup ice water, div. use
2 teaspoons white pepper	2 teaspoons salt
3 teaspoons salt	½ teaspoon white pepper
12 cups water	3 tablespoons sugar
2 cups white wine	3 eggs, beaten
6 to 8 cloves garlic	5 tablespoons matzo meal

Stock: Combine all ingredients for stock in a large pot and bring to a boil. Reduce heat, cover partially and simmer slowly about 1½ hours. Strain the stock; discard fish bones and heads. While the stock is simmering, you can prepare fish mixture.

Fish: Cook carrots in simmering stock until tender, about 15 to 20 minutes. Remove from stock and place in food processor. Process until blended. Transfer to a large mixing bowl.

Work with 1 pound of ground fish at a time. Process 1 pound of fish with 2 to 4 tablespoons ice water for 5 minutes, until smooth. Transfer mixture to mixing bowl. Repeat twice more with remaining fish and ice water. Add salt, pepper, sugar and eggs to fish; mix well. Mixture should be nice and loose. Blend in matzo meal. Fish mixture should not be too hard, but you should be able to form it into balls. You might have to add a little more matzo meal. Have a bowl of ice water ready. The strained fish stock should be boiling on medium heat. Wet your hands. Scoop up a heaping tablespoon of fish about 2½ inches in diameter. Transfer mixture back and forth between your hands to form a ball. Drop into boiling stock. Boil fish balls for 1½ hours on a slow boil, with the cover opened a crack. Remove from heat and et cool. Remove fish balls to another container. Strain soup, saving sliced carrots to garnish. Freeze fish stock for future use.

Yield: 18 servings.   Recipe by Bernie Zucker

Gefilte Fish

This recipe was my great grandmother's, Ethel Budovitch, of Saint John, New Brunswick. It has now been enjoyed by five generations!

8 medium onions, diced
3 tablespoons oil
3 pounds ground fish (e.g., 1 pound doré/pickerel, 1 pound whitefish, 1 pound pike - this is the net weight after filleting and grinding)

4 eggs
2 cups cold water
6 tablespoons matzo meal
3 teaspoons salt (or to taste)
2 teaspoons white pepper
2 tablespoons sugar
2 large carrots, grated

Preheat oven to 325°F. Spray a 10-inch Bundt pan very well with non-stick spray.

In a large skillet, sauté onions in oil on medium heat until soft, but not brown, about 10 minutes. Let cool.

Combine onions, ground fish, eggs, water, matzo meal, salt, pepper and sugar in the large bowl of an electric mixer. Mix on medium speed for 15 minutes, until light. Add grated carrots and mix well.

Pour mixture into prepared Bundt pan and spread evenly. Bake at 325°F for 2¹/₂ hours (see Note). After 1 hour, cover pan with aluminium foil to prevent fish from becoming too brown.

Remove pan from oven and cool for 5 minutes on a rack. Invert carefully onto a serving platter. This is lovely garnished with cherry tomatoes and parsley.

Yield: 16 to 18 servings.

Note: You may have to reduce the temperature by 25°F if your Bundt pan has a dark interior.

Recipe by Sharon London Liss

Fillet of Some Fish

1 onion, thinly sliced	salt and pepper, to taste
1 to 2 cups mushrooms, thinly sliced (and/or any other vegetables you like)	$\frac{1}{4}$ to $\frac{1}{2}$ cup white wine
	1 to 2 tablespoons melted butter
1$\frac{1}{2}$ pounds (750 grams) fish fillets (flounder, sole or whatever kind you like)	$\frac{1}{4}$ to $\frac{1}{2}$ cup seasoned breadcrumbs

Preheat oven to 350°F. Spray an oblong baking dish with non-stick spray.

Spread vegetables over bottom of prepared baking dish. Lay fish fillets on top of veggies; season with salt and pepper. Drizzle wine and butter over fish. Sprinkle with a thin layer of breadcrumbs.

Bake at 350°F for 15 to 20 minutes, until done.

Yield: 4 to 6 servings.

Recipe by Toba Weiss

Tell me what you eat,
I'll tell you who you are.
Anthelme Brillat-Savarin

Fish Fillets in Marinade

1 cup brown sugar, lightly
  packed
½ cup water

2 tablespoons soy sauce
4 fish fillets (8 ounces/250
  grams each)

Combine brown sugar, water and soy sauce in a shallow casserole; mix well. Marinate fish in mixture for 20 minutes.

Spray a large skillet with non-stick spray. Heat on high heat. Remove fillets from marinade and sear about 4 minutes on each side, or until done.

Yield: 4 servings.

Tip: Bragg liquid aminos are a delicious alternative to tamari or soy sauce.

Recipe by G.G.

Fish, to taste right, must swim three times – in water, in butter, and in wine.
Polish Proverb

Oakdale Fish Cakes with Lemon Aïoli

2 small white onions, finely chopped
2 stalks celery, finely chopped
2 teaspoons oil
2 pounds (1 kg) artificial crab meat (pollock)
2 large potatoes, cooked and puréed
juice of 1½ lemons
1 tablespoon Dijon mustard
pinch of salt and pepper

2 tablespoons capers, minced
1 teaspoon chopped parsley
1 teaspoon chopped tarragon
2 tablespoons mayonnaise
1 cup all-purpose flour, seasoned with salt and pepper
3 eggs blended with ½ cup milk
1 cup breadcrumbs
vegetable oil, for frying
Lemon Aïoli (next page)

Heat oil in a small skillet on medium heat. Add onion and celery; lightly sauté for 2 to 3 minutes, until tender but not brown. Set aside to cool.

Place crab in a large bowl and flake with a fork. Add seasoned potato purée, lemon juice, mustard, salt, pepper, capers, parsley and tarragon. Stir in onion, celery and mayonnaise until combined. Form mixture into 4-ounce discs. Freeze fish cakes until firm, but not frozen.

Set up 3 bowls: one with seasoned flour, one with egg/milk mixture and one with breadcrumbs. Pass each fish cake through flour, egg wash and then breadcrumbs.

In a large skillet on medium-high heat, sauté fish cakes in hot oil until golden brown, about 4 minutes per side. Serve with Lemon Aïoli and a small salad to garnish.

Yield: 8 fish cakes.

Recipe by James Saunders, Chef

Lemon Aïoli

2 egg yolks
¼ cup lemon juice
3 cloves garlic purée

½ teaspoon sea salt
pinch of pepper
¾ cup olive oil

Combine egg yolks, lemon juice, garlic, salt, pepper and lemon juice in a food processor. Process until blended, about 15 seconds. Slowly drizzle in olive oil through feed tube to make a thick mayonnaise-like mixture. Can be made in advance and refrigerated.

Yield: about 1 cup.

Recipe by James Saunders, Chef

A nickel will get you on the subway but garlic will get you a seat.

Old New York Proverb

Lemon Halibut with Papaya Salsa

Salsa:
1/2 cup cilantro leaves, roughly chopped
1 cup papaya, cut in cubes
1/4 cup sweet red pepper, diced
1/4 cup red onion, diced
1 small jalapeno pepper, seeded and minced
2 tablespoons freshly squeezed lime juice

Marinade:
3 tablespoons freshly squeezed lemon juice
1 tablespoon grated lemon zest

1 tablespoon olive oil
1 tablespoon grated fresh ginger
3/4 teaspoon freshly ground black pepper
1/2 cup minced fresh cilantro

Halibut and Fennel:
6 halibut steaks (6 ounces/180 grams each), sliced in half lengthwise
3 medium bulbs fennel, trimmed and sliced
9 black or white peppercorns
2/3 cup purified water

Salsa: Combine cilantro with papaya, red pepper, onion, jalapeno and lime juice in a bowl; mix lightly. Cover and refrigerate until ready to serve.

Marinade: Combine lemon juice with lemon zest, olive oil, ginger, pepper and cilantro. Cover and let flavours mingle for at least 2 hours or overnight in the refrigerator.

Preparation: Preheat oven to 400°F. Place fish in a baking pan. Pour marinade over fish, cover with plastic wrap and refrigerate for 20 minutes.

In a large, deep skillet, cook fennel with peppercorns in purified water for 6 to 8 minutes, until just tender, adding more water if necessary.

While fennel is cooking, bake halibut about 5 minutes per side. The halibut should be flaky and white. Drain fennel and arrange a few slices on each plate. Top with halibut and spoon salsa on fish.

Yield: 6 servings.   Recipe by G.G.

Gravlax

1 baby salmon (3½ pounds/ 1.5 kg), filleted	½ cup sugar
1 large bunch of dill	1 to 2 teaspoons coriander seeds
Seasoning Mix:	2 tablespoons crushed peppercorns
½ cup coarse salt	

Place one piece of salmon skin-side down in a large utility dish. Cover with a large bunch of dill.

Combine ingredients for seasoning mix and spread over dill. Place the second fillet on top, skin-side up. Wrap the salmon in cheesecloth for easier turning. Place a heavy weight on top, such as two 48-ounce cans of juice.

Refrigerate for 4 to 5 days, turning salmon over twice a day.

To serve, wipe off the salt mixture and discard dill. Slice diagonally with a sharp knife. Serve on cocktail pumpernickel bread spread with honey mustard. Freezes perfectly!

Yield: 20 to 24 servings.

Recipe by Sharon London Liss

Cedar Plank Salmon with Grainy Pecan Crust

Marinade:
¼ cup vegetable oil
1 lemon
2 cloves garlic purée
1 sprig thyme

4 salmon fillets (6 ounces/
  180 grams each)
2 tablespoons olive oil
pinch of salt and pepper

Crust:
4 tablespoons grainy mustard
20 toasted pecans roughly
  chopped
2 tablespoons chopped parsley
2 tablespoons chopped chives

Combne ingredients for marinade in a shallow bowl. Place salmon fillets in marinade and refrigerate for 24 hours.

Take 4 pieces of cedar plank (roughly 8 inches x 4 inches) and soak them in a bath of warm water for 2 hours prior to cooking.

Preheat oven to 350°F. Sear the salmon in a hot skillet in olive oil for 2 minutes, until golden and crispy on the outside. Only turn the salmon once. Season it with salt and pepper.

Remove cedar planks from the water. Place a salmon fillet on each plank and bake at 350°F for 8 minutes.

Remove planks from oven. Top each fillet with a tablespoon of mustard. Sprinkle with pecans and fresh herbs. Return salmon to oven until cooked, about 6 to 8 minutes longer. (Cooking time will depend on thickness of fish.)

Serve the salmon on the boards for a more creative presentation.

Yield: 4 servings.

Recipe by James Saunders, Chef

Cold Dilled Salmon

1 salmon fillet (2 to 3
  pounds/1 to 1½ kg)
salt and pepper, to taste
¼ cup chopped fresh dill
½ cup white wine

Sauce:
½ cup light mayonnaise
½ cup light sour cream
2 tablespoons additional
  chopped fresh dill

Preheat oven to 425°F.

Sprinkle salmon with salt, pepper and ¼ cup dill. Place in a large sprayed baking dish. Drizzle wine around and over salmon.

Cover and bake at 425°F for 20 minutes, or until done. Cooking time will depend on thickness of fish. Let cool; refrigerate salmon for several hours or overnight. Transfer carefully to a large serving platter.

Sauce: Combine mayonnaise, sour cream and remaining dill in a bowl; mix well. Refrigerate until serving time.

Serve chilled salmon with sauce on the side.

Yield: 6 to 8 servings.

Recipe by Toba Weiss

Dilled Salmon Wellington

6 tablespoons butter, divided use (or olive oil)
10 shallots (about 2 cups, finely chopped)
1/2 cup dry white wine
1/4 teaspoon salt

1 cup fresh dill, finely chopped
8 sheets phyllo pastry
Dijon mustard (optional)
4 salmon fillets (5 ounces/ 150 grams each)

Preheat oven 400°F. Melt 2 tablespoons of butter in a large frying pan over medium heat. Add shallots and stir frequently for 5 minutes. Add wine and salt. Increase heat to medium-high and stir until wine has evaporated, about 8 minutes. Remove pan from heat and stir in dill.

Melt remaining 4 tablespoons butter. Place a sheet of phyllo dough on a flat surface. Spread with a thin layer of mustard. Using a pastry brush, lightly brush phyllo with melted butter. Top with a second sheet of phyllo.

Form each salmon fillet into a rectangle by tucking in the thin end. Place a salmon fillet in the center of phyllo. The long side of salmon should be parallel to the long side of phyllo. Spread a quarter of dill mixture on top and sides of salmon; gently press mixture into salmon.

Bring the two long sides of phyllo together over the top of salmon. Fold them together, accordion-like, until they tightly wrap salmon. You now have a thin long rectangle.

Gently bring up both short ends of phyllo towards the middle of wrapped salmon. Scrunch the ends together so the pastry flares out into ruffles, forming a flower. Place on an ungreased baking sheet and brush with melted butter. Repeat with remaining salmon and phyllo. If making these ahead of time, refrigerate for no more than 4 hours.

Bake in the center of oven at 400°F about 15 minutes, or until golden. Use a wide metal spatula to remove packets from baking sheet.

Yield: 4 servings.

Tip: Makes for elegant dining.   Recipe by G.G.

Oriental Salmon

1 salmon fillet (3 pounds/
  1.4 kg), center cut, skin on

Marinade:
3 tablespoons sesame seeds,
  preferably unhulled
½ cup medium dry sherry
3 tablespoons Oriental
  sesame oil

3 tablespoons dark soy sauce
2 tablespoons minced fresh
  ginger
1 tablespoon minced garlic
½ cup scallions (white part
  only) cut in 1/8th-inch
  rounds (reserve green part
  for Scallion Brushes, below)
lemon twists, for garnish

Rinse salmon under cold water; pat dry. Place skin-side down on an oiled, oblong shallow baking pan.

Combine marinade ingredients in a bowl and mix well. Spoon the marinade over salmon. Marinate at room temperature for 1 hour.

Preheat broiler. Broil salmon 4 inches from the heat for 10 to 12 minutes, or until cooked through. (If salmon is more than 1½ inches thick, broil it first for 10 minutes, then bake it at 400°F for an additional 5 minutes.) Do not turn salmon over. If juices evaporate, splash with a little additional sherry.

Remove salmon to a serving platter, using 2 wide spatulas. Garnish with Scallion Brushes and lemon twists. Serve hot or at room temperature.

Yield: 6 to 8 servings.

Scallion Brushes: Use green part of scallions; trim off roots. Scallions should be 5 to 6 inches long. With a sharp knife, cut several slits about 1 inch long at both ends of scallions; leave at least ¾ inch uncut in the center of each piece. Soak in ice water for 15 minutes. Pat dry.

Recipe by Vera Finkelstein

Salmon with Limes

2 limes
3 salmon fillets (5 ounces/
150 grams each), 1 inch
thick
1 tablespoon grated fresh
ginger
$\frac{1}{8}$ teaspoon salt

$\frac{1}{8}$ teaspoon pepper
2 tablespoons toasted sesame
oil
2 cups trimmed small green
beans
additional lime wedges,
for serving

Preheat oven to 450°F.

Place a large sheet of heavy-duty aluminium foil on a flat surface. Grate zest from lime; measure 2 teaspoons and set aside.

Slice limes; arrange slices in a single layer on foil. Place fish in a single layer on top of limes.

In a small bowl, combine reserved lime zest with ginger, salt, pepper and sesame oil; mix well. Brush mixture generously over fish and wrap it tightly.

Bake at 450°F for 10 to 15 minutes, until cooked through. Meanwhile, cook beans for 4 to 5 minutes in boiling salted water; drain well.

Arrange cooked beans and fish attractively in a serving dish. Serve with additional lime wedges for squeezing over cooked fish.

Yield: 3 servings.

Recipe by G.G.

Salmon with Maple Glaze

1 salmon fillet (2½ pounds/ 1.2 kg) center cut, skin on
1 bunch scallions, green part

Marinade:
4 tablespoons fresh lemon juice, divided use

1 cup pure maple syrup
3 tablespoons soy sauce
2 tablespoons fresh ginger, peeled and finely grated
1½ teaspoons minced garlic
salt and pepper to taste

In a small heavy saucepan, combine maple syrup with 3 tablespoons of lemon juice, soy sauce, ginger, garlic, salt and pepper. Bring to a boil. Reduce heat and simmer, uncovered, until reduced to about 1 cup, about 30 minutes; stir occasionally. Let cool.

Preheat oven to 350°F. Lightly oil a shallow baking pan large enough to hold salmon.

Arrange scallions in baking pan to form a bed for salmon. Drizzle ½ cup of maple glaze over salmon. Bake at 350°F for 20 to 25 minutes. Baking time depends on thickness of fish.

In a small saucepan, heat the remaining ½ cup of maple glaze over low heat until heated through. This will be used as a sauce. Stir in the remaining tablespoon lemon juice. Remove pan from heat, cover sauce and keep warm.

Cut salmon crosswise into 6 pieces. Drizzle warm sauce over salmon.

Yield: 6 servings.

Tip: Maple glaze may be made 2 days ahead, covered and refrigerated. Bring glaze to room temperature before proceeding with recipe.

Recipe by G.G.

Salmon with Oregano and Lime Sauce

This is also delicious with Arctic char or sea bass.

1 salmon fillet (about 2½ pounds/1.2 kg) or 4 to 6 individual fillets 2 to 3 tablespoons olive oil 1 cup chopped fresh oregano	4 cloves minced fresh garlic ¼ cup lime juice salt and freshly ground pepper lime wedges or slices, to garnish

Preheat oven to 450°F.

Wipe fish with damp paper towels and pat dry. Remove fat from bottom of salmon fillets. Make at least 1 to 2 slashes in each piece so the marinade can penetrate.

Rub fish with olive oil. Mix together, oregano and minced garlic. Spread mixture over fish, placing a generous amount into slashes. Marinate at room temperature for 30 minutes. Sprinkle with lime juice and season with salt and pepper to taste.

Place fish in a foil-lined, shallow baking dish. (For salmon, wrap it completely in foil; for other types of fish, bake uncovered.)

Bake at 450°F allowing 10 minutes per inch of thickness measured at its thickest point. (Bake it about 12 to 15 minutes, then take a peek.) If necessary, bake a few minutes longer.

Yield: 4 to 6 servings.

Tip: You may want to garnish the salmon with additional fresh herbs.

Recipe by G.G.

Steamed Salmon with Salsa Verde

Salsa Verde:
1 handful Italian parsley
1 handful fresh
   coriander/cilantro
3 cloves garlic, peeled
1 shallot, peeled

2 tablespoons capers
2 tablespoons caper brine
2 tablespoons lemon juice
4 to 5 tablespoons olive oil
$\frac{1}{2}$ to 1 teaspoon salt

Chop all the ingredients in a blender or food processor until coarsely chopped; do not overprocess. You don't want the texture to be too smooth.

Steamed Salmon:
4 salmon fillets (6 ounces/180 grams each), skin on

Use an electric steamer. Spray pan with non-stick spray. Lay salmon fillets skin-side down in pan and place in steamer. Set timer to 6 minutes on cooking cycle and press start.

When the timer beeps, check for doneness. Salmon will continue to cook for about 5 minutes after it's removed from the steamer. You don't want it too well done. Pierce gently with a knife: if there's a bit of pink at the center, it's done. If there's deep pink, put it back in the steamer and steam 3 minutes longer.

Serve this topped with Salsa Verde.

Yield: 4 servings.

Recipe by Lisa Slater

Wabi-Sabi Salmon

4 to 6 salmon fillets (preferably wild-caught organic salmon)	soy sauce, to taste
	grated fresh ginger
	Dijon mayonnaise
1 bag of wasabi peas (dried peas flavoured with wasabi)	pickled ginger, for garnish

Preheat oven to 450°F, or preheat grill.

Crush the bag of wasabi peas into crumbs. (You can do this right in the bag.) Dip salmon fillets into soy sauce mixed with fresh ginger. Brush with Dijon mayonnaise. Now sprinkle the crushed peas generously on the fillets.

Bake uncovered at 450°F for 15 minutes, or grill about 8 minutes per side. Garnish with pickled ginger.

Yield: 4 to 6 servings.

Recipe by Richard J. Lewis

Grilled Tuna with Mango Salad

1 large mango, peeled, pitted
   and cut into ¼-inch wide
   strips
¾ cup chopped red onion
½ of a red bell pepper,
   chopped
3 tablespoons chopped fresh
   cilantro/coriander

2 tablespoons rice vinegar
2 tablespoons olive oil
salt and pepper to taste
4 tuna steaks, about 1 inch
   thick (6 ounces/180 grams
   each)
1 tablespoon vegetable oil

Combine mango, onion, red pepper, cilantro, rice vinegar and olive oil in a medium bowl; season with salt and pepper.

Preheat grill on medium-high heat (or preheat broiler). Brush tuna with oil. Grill or broil until just opaque in the center, about 4 minutes per side. Do not overcook.

Divide mango salad among 4 plates and top with tuna.

Yield: 4 servings.

Note: Divine if you like tuna.

Recipe by G.G.

Sesame Tuna

2 tuna steaks (very fresh) (1 to 1½ inches thick)	½ cup sesame seeds
½ cup soya sauce (I use Bragg liquid aminos)	4 tablespoons pesto sauce (homemade or store-bought)

Dip tuna steaks into soya sauce and sesame seeds, coating both sides.

Heat a non-stick frying pan on high heat. Sear tuna steaks quickly on each side. Lower the heat and cook gently (the centre of the fish should be red).

Remove from heat and spread with pesto.

Yield: 2 hearty servings. This is such a treat!!!

Recipe by G.G.

After dinner sit a while,
and after supper walk a mile.
English Saying

Tuna, Lemon and Caper Sauce

This tasty recipe comes from Joie Warner.

1 can (6 ounces/170 grams) chunk or solid white tuna in olive oil, drained
1 large clove garlic, finely chopped
grated zest of 1 medium lemon
2 tablespoons fresh lemon juice
¼ cup olive oil
2 tablespoons capers, drained
½ teaspoon salt
pepper, to taste
1 package (8 ounces/250 grams) pasta (e.g., medium shells, penne rigate, rigatoni or linguine)
¼ cup chopped fresh parsley
grated Parmesan cheese

In a pasta bowl, break up tuna with a fork. Add garlic, lemon zest, lemon juice, olive oil, capers, salt and freshly ground pepper. Mix well.

Cook pasta in a large pot of boiling salted water according to package directions, until al dente. Drain well and add to sauce. Sprinkle with parsley and toss. Serve topped with Parmesan cheese.

Yield: 2 to 4 servings.

Tip: Enhanced with lemon, this robust sauce is also delicious with black olives and a large ripe tomato, seeded and diced.

Recipe by G.G.

MEAT AND POULTRY

Calves' Liver with Onions

1 tablespoon olive oil (plus more oil as needed)	salt and black pepper, to taste
2 large onions, thinly sliced	3 tablespoons sherry vinegar
2 pounds (1 kg) calves' liver ($\frac{1}{2}$ inch thick)	3 tablespoons chicken broth
	2 tablespoons chopped Italian parsley

Heat oil in a large skillet on medium heat. Add onions and cook slowly until golden, stirring occasionally, about 20 minutes.

Remove onions from skillet with a slotted spoon and place in a small bowl; cover with foil to keep warm.

Cook liver, 2 slices at a time, about $1\frac{1}{2}$ minutes per side for medium-rare, adding oil only if needed. Season liver with salt and pepper to taste. Cut each slice on the diagonal into 6 pieces. Arrange on a platter and cover loosely with foil to keep warm.

Add vinegar and broth to skillet. Bring to a boil, scraping up any browned bits. Add the reserved onions and heat on medium for 1 minute to warm them through.

Spoon the onions over liver. Sprinkle with chopped parsley.

Yield: 6 servings.

Tip: If you are concerned about cholesterol, make this dish for special occasions.

Recipe by G.G.

Spanish Tongue

1 pickled tongue (about 4 pounds/1.8 kg)	cold water, to cover

Place tongue in a large kettle of cold water. Bring to a boil; skim off scum that forms on top. Cover pot and cook tongue on low to medium heat for approximately 2 hours, until tender. Cool in stock.

When cooled, remove skin and any excess fat. Cover and refrigerate. Prepare sauce.

Spanish Sauce:	½ green pepper, sliced
2 tablespoons oil	1 bottle (10 ounces/300 ml)
2 onions, sliced	chili sauce
3 carrots, sliced	½ teaspoon lemon juice
4 ribs celery, sliced	2 tablespoons brown sugar
1 can (28 ounces/796 ml) stewed tomatoes	1½ cups sliced mushrooms
	1 cup sliced pitted olives

Preheat oven to 350°F. Slice cooked tongue and place in shallow casserole dish. Heat oil in a large skillet on low heat. Add onions, cover and let them sweat for 5 minutes, until softened. Add carrots, celery and green pepper. Cover and steam about 5 minutes, until slightly softened.

Add stewed tomatoes, chili sauce, lemon juice and sugar. Bring to a boil and cook for 5 minutes. Pour over sliced tongue. Stir in mushrooms and olives.

Bake uncovered at 350°F for 30 to 45 minutes.

Yield: 6 to 8 servings.

Recipe by Ronda Roth

Rack of Lamb

2 racks of lamb, well trimmed   1 clove garlic, minced
¼ cup Dijon mustard   ½ teaspoon dried marjoram or
1½ teaspoons light soy sauce   thyme, crumbled
1½ teaspoons dark soy sauce   ⅛ teaspoon ground ginger

Preheat oven to 400°F.

Arrange racks of lamb on a foil-lined baking sheet, bone-side down. Combine mustard, soy sauces, garlic, marjoram and ginger in a small bowl, blending well. Coat the lamb thoroughly with this mixture.

Roast lamb uncovered at 400°F until tender, about 15 to 20 minutes. Transfer to a serving platter. Serve with mint sauce, if desired.

Yield: 4 servings.

Recipe by Brooky Robins

Roast Leg of Lamb with Currant Jelly

1 leg of lamb, well trimmed (3
  to 4 pounds/1.5 to 2 kg)
coarse salt
juice of a lemon
garlic salt, to taste

pepper, to taste
paprika, to taste
1 jar (8 ounce/250 ml) currant
  jelly
$\frac{1}{2}$ cup sherry

Preheat oven to 350°F.

Rub meat with coarse salt and lemon juice; let stand 10 to 15 minutes. Rinse meat thoroughly and pat dry.

Sprinkle with garlic salt, pepper and paprika. Place the roast on a rack in a large roasting pan. Roast uncovered at 350°F until nicely browned, calculating 20 to 25 minutes per pound as your cooking time.

Mix currant jelly with sherry. During the last half hour, brush roast with jelly mixture; baste several times until roast is done.

Yield: 6 to 8 servings.

Recipe by Phyllis Crystal

Veal Tenderloin With Herb Crust

1 tablespoon extra-virgin olive oil
1 teaspoon sea salt
1 teaspoon black pepper
1 kilogram (2.2 pounds) veal tenderloin (boneless veal roast can be substituted)

3 tablespoons Dijon mustard
2 teaspoons minced fresh sage
2 teaspoons minced fresh thyme
2 teaspoons minced fresh parsley
1 cup sweet red wine

Preheat oven to 475°F.

Mix oil with salt and pepper in a small bowl. Rub mixture over veal roast on all sides.

Heat a heavy skillet over high heat. Add veal and quickly sear on all sides until golden brown.

Remove veal from skillet and place on a rack in a large roasting pan. Coat the veal with Dijon mustard and herbs. Pour wine into the bottom of roasting pan.

Roast uncovered at 475°F for 15 minutes. Reduce temperature to 350°F and cook another 25 minutes.

Remove meat from oven and let rest for 5 to 10 minutes. Slice meat and place on a serving platter. Pour pan juices over meat and serve.

Yield: 4 to 6 servings.

Recipe by Joe Rovito, Chef

Vitel Tonné

This is also known as Vitello Tonnato.

3 pounds (1.4 kg) veal shoulder roast	8 or 9 peppercorns
2 carrots	1 bay leaf
2 sticks of celery	1 cup white wine
1 large onion	1 teaspoon salt (or 1 chicken bouillon cube)
3 or 4 sprigs parsley	water

Place the above ingredients in a large pot, adding just enough water to cover. Bring to a boil; reduce heat and cook slowly, covered, for about $1\frac{1}{2}$ to 2 hours. Remove meat from broth and set aside. Discard the cooked vegetables. Bring broth back to a boil; cook uncovered on high heat until reduced to about 1 cup. Add meat back to broth and let cool. Refrigerate overnight.

Sauce:	$\frac{3}{4}$ cup canola mayonnaise
2 cans (7 ounces/200 grams each) tuna packed in oil (preferable Italian)	$\frac{1}{2}$ cup of white bread, soaked in water and squeezed dry
1 tablespoon margarine	$\frac{1}{2}$ cup reserved broth from meat (or more if necessary)
4 to 5 anchovy fillets (or 1 tablespoon anchovy paste)	$\frac{1}{2}$ cup lemon juice

Put all ingredients for sauce in a food processor and process until very smooth, adding more broth, if necessary.

Garnish: 3 tablespoons small capers, 6 to 8 black olives, pitted and cut in slivers (or 2 tablespoons olive paste)

Assembly: Cut roast in very thin slices, trimming off any fat. Pour a little of the sauce onto a large serving platter and spread it evenly. Arrange a layer of meat slices on the sauce; top the meat with a layer of sauce. Do not put more than one layer of meat on each platter. Cover tightly and refrigerate. May be made 2 to 3 days ahead of time. Bring to room temperature before serving. Decorate with capers and olives.

Yield: 12 to 16 servings. Recipe by Fanny Cava

Roasted Shoulder of Veal

4 to 5 pounds (1.8 to 2.3 kg)
boneless veal shoulder, tied
(or a filet of veal)
1 clove garlic, cut in slivers
1 teaspoon dried herb mixture
(your favourite)

¼ cup Dijon mustard
salt and pepper, to taste
6 tablespoons seasoned olive
or grapeseed oil
¾ cup dry white wine

Preheat oven to 350°F.

Cut tiny slits in veal with sharp knife and insert garlic slivers. Set the roast on a rack in a shallow baking pan. Rub mustard all over veal; sprinkle with herb mixture, salt and pepper. Drizzle oil over veal. Pour wine into pan.

Roast uncovered at 350°F for 2 hours and 15 minutes, basting often. (Calculate 25 to 30 minutes per pound for the cooking time. A filet of veal only needs 20 minutes per pound.)

Remove from oven and let stand for 20 minutes before carving. Serve gravy from pan juices with veal.

Yield: 6 to 8 servings.

Recipe by G.G.

Osso Bucco with Lemon Gremolata

8 thick slices veal shank, each tied with a string (1½ to 2 inches thick)
salt and black pepper, to taste
all-purpose flour (or corn meal)
2 tablespoons olive oil
2 tablespoons margarine (or Earth Balance buttery spread)
2 medium onions, finely chopped
1 stalk celery, finely chopped
12 baby carrots
5 large cloves garlic, minced
1 cup dry white wine
¾ to 1 cup chicken or vegetable broth
1 can (28 ounces/796 ml) tomatoes, drained & chopped
2 whole fresh basil leaves
1½ teaspoons dried thyme (or 2 fresh whole sprigs of thyme)
2 bay leaves

Lightly sprinkle veal shanks with salt and pepper on both sides. Coat on all sides with flour; shake off excess. In a large skillet, heat oil over medium-high heat. Brown the veal on both sides. Remove from pan and transfer to a heavy pot or ovenproof casserole.

In the same skillet, melt margarine on medium heat. Add onions, celery, carrots and garlic. Sauté until softened, 5 to 10 minutes. Add wine, chicken broth, drained tomatoes, basil, thyme and bay leaves to skillet. Stir to combine. Pour over veal. Season again to taste.

Cover and cook on top of stove on low heat for 2 to 3 hours, until very tender, basting occasionally. (Or place in a 325°F oven for 2 to 3 hours.) Discard bay leaves. Remove strings from veal and place on platter. Spoon sauce over veal and sprinkle with Gremolata.

Yield: 6 to 8 servings. This dish can be made 1 to 2 days in advance.

Gremolata:
1 tablespoon grated lemon zest
1 clove garlic, minced
¼ cup fresh parsley, chopped

In a bowl, combine lemon zest, garlic and parsley; mix well. (Don't forget to add the Gremolata - it really boosts the flavour!)

Recipe by G.G.

Boeuf Bourguignon

2 to 3 tablespoons canola oil
2 medium onions, sliced
½ pound (250 grams/8 ounces) mushrooms, quartered
1½ pounds (750 grams) stewing beef
salt, pepper and garlic, to taste
1 to 1½ cups Burgundy wine (approximately)
¼ cup chopped fresh parsley, to taste
2 cups tiny white pearl onions, fresh or frozen
2 teaspoons flour dissolved in 1 tablespoon cold water

Heat oil in a large heavy-bottomed pot on medium heat. Add onions and mushrooms and sauté until tender, about 8 to 10 minutes. Remove from pot and set aside.

Brown beef slowly in hot oil on all sides, about 8 to 10 minutes. Add wine (you will need enough to cover the beef). Add reserved onions and mushrooms along with seasonings.

Simmer partially covered about 1 hour. Add white onions and continue cooking until meat is tender, about 1½ hours longer.

If there is too much liquid, uncover and cook for a few minutes longer, until reduced. Stir in flour mixture to slightly thicken the sauce so it coats a spoon.

Yield: 4 to 6 servings.

Note: I prefer frozen onions because I don't have to clean them!

Recipe by Toba Weiss

Glorious Stew

1 cup dried navy beans	1 strip of kishka (or 4 large
1 cup dried kidney beans	veal or turkey hot dogs),
6 cups cold water	cut in chunks
1 tablespoon grapeseed oil	1½ tablespoons salt (see Tip
1 large onion, sliced	below)
5 cloves garlic, chopped	pepper, to taste
5 peeled potatoes, cut in	3 tablespoons paprika
chunks	1 tablespoon garlic pepper
3 strips flanken, cut in chunks	2 to 3 cups chicken broth
1 cup pearl barley, rinsed and	(enough to cover all
drained	ingredients)

Soak navy beans and kidney beans in cold water overnight. Rinse and drain well.

Preheat oven to 275°F. Place all ingredients in a large ovenproof pot. Cover with broth.

Cover tightly and place in oven from late afternoon until noon the next day. Check in the morning and if it appears to be dry, add more boiling water.

Yield: about 15 cups.

Note: Barley absorbs salt and pepper, so you have to use much more seasoning than you would normally use.

Recipe by G.G.

Grilled Miami Ribs

½ cup red wine
½ cup lemon juice
½ cup soy sauce
⅓ cup brown sugar, lightly packed
6 cloves fresh garlic, minced

1 tablespoon mustard (e.g., Dijon)
2 pounds (1 kg) Miami ribs (about 8 to 12 strips, ¼ inch thick)

In a bowl, combine wine, lemon juice, soy sauce, brown sugar, mustard and garlic. Mix well. Pour marinade into a shallow casserole and add ribs. Marinate at least 2 hours (or overnight) in the refrigerator.

Drain ribs and pat dry. Strain marinade into a saucepan and cook for 10 minutes, until syrupy. It should be reduced to about ½ cup. Let cool.

Grill ribs about one minute on each side. Brush with some of the boiled marinade and grill about 3 minutes longer on each side, brushing with marinade each time. Brush one last time after removing ribs from grill.

Yield: 4 servings.

Note: Miami ribs should be only ¼-inch thick for broiling or grilling. If they are any thicker, they need to be cooked like short ribs (i.e., they should be braised with vegetables and some liquid, until very tender, about 2½ hours).

Recipe by G.G.

Filet Roast

1 filet roast (4 to 5 pounds/	½ cup wine vinegar
1.8 to 2.3 kg)	¼ cup soy sauce
salt and pepper, to taste	¼ cup salad oil
Marinade:	¼ cup corn syrup
2 cloves garlic	½ teaspoon dry mustard

Sprinkle meat with salt and pepper on all sides. Place in a large casserole dish.

Combine marinade ingredients and blend well. Pour over meat. Cover and marinate for several hours (or overnight) in the refrigerator.

Two hours before roasting, bring meat to room temperature. Score fat by slashing it in several places with a sharp knife. If the meat does not have a layer of fat, rub it well with oil. Place fat-side up on a rack in a shallow roasting pan. Insert a meat thermometer in the thickest part of the roast.

Preheat oven to 450°F. Roast uncovered for 15 minutes. Reduce temperature to 350°F and continue roasting meat for another 1½ to 2 hours, until thermometer registers 5 degrees below the desired doneness.

Remove from oven and let rest for 20 minutes before carving. This allows the juices to be absorbed by the meat.

Yield: 8 to 10 servings.

Note: This roast is best served rare or medium rare.

Recipe by Ronda Roth

Janna and Brooky's Brisket

1 beef brisket (5 pounds/ 2.3 kg)	³/₄ cup orange juice
1 package dehydrated onion soup mix	1 tablespoon soy sauce
	¹/₈ cup teriyaki sauce
2 large white cooking onions	1 clove garlic, finely minced

Preheat oven to 350°F. Spray a large roasting pan with non-stick spray.

Rub brisket all over with dried onion soup. Place half of onions in bottom of roasting pan. Place the brisket, fat-side up, on top of onions. Cover with remaining onions.

In a small bowl, combine orange juice, soy sauce, teriyaki sauce and garlic; pour over brisket. Cover pan tightly with foil.

Bake at 350°F for 4 hours, or until tender, basting frequently. Cover pan tightly between bastings.

Yield: 8 servings.

Note: Carrots and potatoes may be added during the last hour of cooking.

Recipe by Brooky Robins

Pepper Steak

2 pounds (1 kg) thinly sliced
  steak, well trimmed
4 teaspoons oil
1/2 cup scallions or onions,
  thinly sliced
2 cloves garlic, minced
2 or 3 green peppers, thinly
  sliced

1 cup sliced celery
1 1/2 cups beef broth
  (I use Carmel beef-flavoured
  soup mix plus water)
2 tablespoons cornstarch
1/4 cup water
2 tablespoons soy sauce

Cut steak into narrow strips. Heat oil in a large skillet on medium-high heat. Brown the steak on all sides in oil until no traces of pink remain, about 5 to 7 minutes.

Add scallions, garlic, green peppers and celery. Cook 5 minutes longer, stirring occasionally. Add beef broth. Cover and cook over low heat for 10 minutes.

In a small bowl, mix cornstarch with water and soy sauce until smooth. Slowly add to skillet, stirring constantly, until sauce comes to a boil. Cook 2 minutes longer. Serve with rice.

Yield: 4 servings.

Recipe by Bea Myers

Marinade for Meats

1½ cups oil
½ cup soy sauce
½ cup Worcestershire sauce
1 tablespoon ground black
   pepper
½ cup wine vinegar

1 clove garlic, crushed
½ cup fresh lemon juice
1½ teaspoons dried parsley
   flakes
2½ teaspoons salt
2 tablespoons dry mustard

Combine all ingredients together in a large bowl and mix well.

Use as a marinade for beef tenderloin roast or filet mignon steaks. Marinate for 24 hours for best results.

Yield: about 3½ cups.

Recipe by Marilyn Himmel

The belly rules the mind.
Spanish Proverb

Chili

6 tablespoons olive oil	3 tablespoons Worcestershire
3 onions, chopped	sauce
1 green pepper, chopped	1 teaspoon salt
1 cup celery, chopped	1 tablespoon chili powder
3 cloves garlic, minced	1 teaspoon dried oregano
2 pounds (1 kg) lean ground	1 teaspoon dried thyme
beef	1 tablespoon dried basil
1 can (28 ounces/796 ml)	1 teaspoon cumin seeds
tomatoes	2 teaspoons hot mustard
1 can (5½ ounces/156 ml)	1 can (19 ounces/540 ml) kid-
tomato paste	ney beans, rinsed and
1 bay leaf	drained

Heat oil in a large, heavy-bottomed pot on medium heat. Add onions, green pepper, celery and garlic. Sauté for 6 to 8 minutes, until softened.

Add ground beef and brown slowly, stirring often, until no traces of pink remain, about 10 minutes.

Add remaining ingredients except kidney beans. Bring mixture to a boil, reduce heat, cover and simmer for 2 hours, stirring occasionally.

Add kidney beans and cook 5 to 10 minutes longer, until heated through. Serve over rice or pasta.

Yield: 6 to 8 servings.

Recipe by Diane Oille

Pauline's Sweet and Sour Meatballs

Sauce:
1 tablespoon oil
2 medium onions, diced
salt and pepper
1 tablespoon brown sugar
1 can (28 ounces/796 ml)
  whole tomatoes
1 can (14 ounces/398 ml)
  tomato sauce
juice of half a lemon

additional brown sugar,
  to taste

Meat:
4 slices white bread, crusts
  removed
salt and pepper, to taste
3 pounds (1.4 kg) ground meat
  (chuck, veal and/or chicken)

Sauce: Heat oil in a large pot on medium-low heat. Add onions and sprinkle lightly with salt and pepper. Gently sauté until golden, about 10 minutes. Add brown sugar, stirring until dissolved. Add tomatoes and tomato sauce. Let sauce boil gently, stirring occasionally.

Meat: Soak bread in cold water to cover. Crumble it with your hands. Add soaked bread, salt and pepper to meat, continuing to work with your hands until meat is a smooth consistency, with no signs of bread visible. Form into balls, wetting your hands for easier handling. Add meatballs to boiling sauce.

Reduce heat to simmer. Cover pot and simmer slowly for 1½ hours. Add lemon juice and additional brown sugar to taste. Serve over rice.

Notes: Matzo meal can be substituted for bread. Work into meat the same as above. This dish may be made ahead and reheated in a casserole in the oven. Freezes well. Defrost before reheating.

Yield: 8 servings.

Recipe by Pauline Toker

Agristada

These delicious meatballs are cooked in a Turkish sauce.
You can substitute ground fish or chicken for veal.

Meat:
1 pound (500 grams) ground
  veal
2 tablespoons chopped parsley
2 slices bread, soaked and
  squeezed dry
1 egg
pinch of salt and pepper

Sauce:
1½ cups water
3 tablespoons vegetable oil
juice of a lemon (freshly
  squeezed is best)

2 tablespoons flour
½ cup additional lemon juice
2 egg yolks
pinch of salt
small pinch of sugar

Meat: Mix veal with parsley, bread, egg, salt and pepper in a mixing bowl. Form into small meatballs, wetting your hands for easier handling.

Sauce: In a pot over high heat, combine water, oil and juice of a lemon. Heat to boiling. Add meatballs. Reduce heat to medium and cook meatballs about 15 minutes. Remove meatballs from sauce and set aside.

Strain sauce and cool slightly. Put sauce into a blender with flour, ½ cup lemon juice, egg yolks and salt. Blend well. Pour sauce back into the pot and cook slowly until it thickens, stirring often.

Add cooked meatballs and sugar. Cook 10 minutes longer, stirring often to prevent sauce from becoming lumpy.

Yield: 4 servings.

Recipe by Fanny Cava

A Favourite Meat Loaf

Meat:
10 to 12 garlic croutons
$\frac{1}{2}$ teaspoon black pepper
$\frac{1}{4}$ teaspoon cayenne pepper
1 teaspoon dried oregano
1 teaspoon dried thyme
$\frac{1}{2}$ onion, chopped
1 carrot, peeled and chopped
3 whole cloves garlic
$\frac{1}{2}$ of a red pepper
$1\frac{1}{4}$ pounds (600 grams)
  ground veal

$1\frac{1}{4}$ pounds (600 grams)
  ground chuck
$1\frac{1}{2}$ teaspoons Kosher salt
1 egg

Glaze:
$\frac{1}{2}$ cup ketchup
1 tablespoon ground cumin
dash Worcestershire sauce
dash hot pepper sauce
1 tablespoon honey

eheat oven to 325°F. Line a large rimmed baking sheet with archment paper.

eat: Combine croutons, pepper, cayenne, oregano and thyme in a od processor. Pulse with quick on/offs to make fine crumbs. Transfer ixture to a large bowl. Combine onion, carrot, garlic and red pepper in od processor. Pulse until finely chopped, but not puréed. Add to umbs.

ld ground veal, chuck, salt and egg to crumb mixture. Combine oroughly without squeezing the meat.Form mixture into a loaf shape 1 prepared baking sheet.

ake at 325°F for 10 minutes. Meanwhile, prepare glaze.

aze: In a small bowl, combine ketchup, cumin, Worcestershire sauce, ot pepper sauce and honey; mix well. Brush onto meat loaf and ontinue baking for another 80 minutes. Total baking time will be about /2 hours.

eld: 10 to 12 servings.

Recipe by G.G.

Ydessa's Veal Patties (Kolkletten)

*My mother, Ydessa, would chop these ingredients together
with a hackmesser (cleaver). She always maintained,
"Better to chop the meal yourself because you never know what
the butcher puts in the minced meat. If you use store-bought
ground veal, do it at your own risk!"*

1 pound (500 grams) boneless veal shoulder	1 large clove of garlic
1 egg	salt and black pepper, to taste
1 thick slice stale challah	fresh chopped rosemary

Combine all ingredients and mix well. Form into balls about the size of meatballs. Flatten to about ½-inch thickness, which would make them less than 2 inches in diameter.

Broil until crispy.

Yield: 3 servings.

Note: Ydessa Birnbaum sailed to Canada on the S.S. Pulaski in July of 1930. Her kitchen, like that of her mother's, was Kosher and she cooked in a salty Russian style. Only the finest quality available meat and poultry were served and sugar was anathema in anything but desserts.

Recipe by Rosalie Sharp

Grilled Chicken Burgers

2 pounds (1 kg) ground chicken	1 tablespoon reduced-sodium
3 tablespoons grainy-style	soy sauce
Dijon mustard	2 teaspoons Worcestershire
3 tablespoons minced green	sauce
onion (white part only)	salt and pepper to taste

Combine ground chicken with remaining ingredients. Using your hands, mix until well blended.

Refrigerate mixture for 10 to 15 minutes so it will be easier to handle. Form mixture into 6 patties.

To grill: Preheat barbeque. Grill patties for 5 to 6 minutes per side, until cooked through but not overdone.

To broil: Preheat broiler. Broil patties 4 inches from heat for 5 to 6 minutes per side, until cooked through, but not overdone.

Yield: 6 patties.

Note: For firmer patties, add 3 tablespoons of whole-grain bread crumbs to mixture.

Recipe by Lois Friedman Fine

Lemon Chicken Zucchini Burgers

1 medium zucchini	1 pound (500 grams) lean
1 egg	ground chicken or turkey
finely grated zest of ½ lemon	¼ cup bread crumbs (or 1
½ teaspoon salt	slice bread, finely crumbled)
¼ teaspoon freshly ground	1 green onion, thinly sliced
black pepper	

If using an outdoor or indoor grill, spray racks with non-stick spray. Preheat grill or oven broiler.

Grate 1 cup of zucchini. Using your hands, squeeze out as much liquid as possible.

In a large bowl, whisk egg with lemon zest, salt and pepper. Add zucchini, ground chicken, bread crumbs and green onion. Mix well, using either a wooden spoon or your hands. Form into 4 burgers, each about 1 inch thick.

Place on preheated grill and cook until well done, about 6 to 8 minutes per side.

Serve in warm rolls, nan or focaccia and top with a dab of Dijon mustard.

Yield: 4 burgers.

Recipe by G.G.

Turkey Burgers

1 pound (500 grams) ground turkey breast
¼ cup finely shredded carrot
¼ cup finely shredded zucchini
¼ cup finely chopped mushrooms

2 tablespoons dehydrated onion flakes
¼ teaspoon paprika
¼ teaspoon freshly ground pepper
2 tablespoons soy sauce

In a large bowl, place all ingredients and mix together just until combined. Chill 1 hour or more.

If using an outdoor or indoor grill, spray racks with non-stick spray. Preheat grill or oven broiler. Grill or broil until done, about 5 to 6 minutes per side.

These can be served on a bun with your favourite accompaniments.

Yield: 4 patties.

Recipe by Nancy Posluns

Lemon Turkey

1 boneless, skinless turkey
  breast (2 pounds/1 kg)
whole wheat or all-purpose
  flour, for coating
2 tablespoons olive oil
2 cloves garlic, minced

$\frac{1}{4}$ to $\frac{1}{2}$ cup fresh chopped
  parsley
1 slice fresh ginger, minced
$\frac{1}{4}$ to $\frac{1}{2}$ cup lemon juice
$\frac{1}{4}$ to $\frac{1}{2}$ cup white wine

Slice turkey breast into half-inch slices. Pound until about $\frac{1}{4}$ inch thick. Coat each slice lightly with flour.

Heat oil in a large skillet on medium-high heat. Add turkey slices, parsley, garlic and ginger; sauté until turkey is lightly browned, about 3 to 4 minutes per side.

Pour off the oil and add lemon juice and white wine. Heat until bubbling, stirring occasionally.

Yield: 4 to 6 servings.

Note: This makes a very light dinner. I also use same recipe for chicken and fish.

Recipe by Rosalie Sharp

Chicken or Vegetarian Cacciatore

6 boneless skinless single chicken breasts (or 2 pounds/1 kg firm tofu)
2 tablespoons olive oil
1 large onion, chopped
2 cloves garlic, finely chopped
salt and freshly ground black pepper
1 can (28 ounces/796 ml) diced tomatoes
1 small can (3/4 cup) tomato juice
2 green peppers, coarsely chopped
2 red peppers, coarsely chopped
2 yellow peppers, coarsely chopped
red pepper flakes, optional (it really adds some zing!)
1 tablespoon minced fresh basil

If using chicken breasts, rinse and pat dry. Slice chicken or tofu into long strips.

In a large skillet on medium-high heat, add olive oil, onion and garlic. Stir-fry until oil starts to get hot and onions start to sizzle slightly. Add chicken or tofu strips; season with salt and pepper. Stir-fry until chicken or tofu is lightly browned, about 5 minutes.

Reduce heat to medium and add diced tomatoes, tomato juice and peppers. Add a little more salt and red pepper flakes. Mix well. Cover pan and bring sauce to a boil, stirring occasionally. Reduce heat to low and cook 20 minutes longer, until peppers are tender and sauce thickens. Serve over rice or egg noodles.

Yield: 6 servings.

Recipe by Paula Carello

Baked Chicken

Chicken:
3 skinless, boneless single
  chicken breasts
3 skinless, boneless chicken
  thighs
3 skinless chicken legs

¾ cup all-purpose flour
  seasoned with salt, pepper
  and paprika
2 tablespoons vegetable oil
  (plus more if needed)

Chicken: Preheat oven to 350°F. Rinse chicken pieces and pat dry. Lightly coat chicken with seasoned flour. Heat oil in a large skillet on medium-high heat. Add chicken breasts and sauté until they develop a light brown color on both sides, about 3 minutes per side. Remove from skillet and set aside. Repeat with chicken thighs and legs, adding more oil if needed. It may take 4 minutes per side for the dark meat.

Vegetables:
2 tablespoons vegetable oil
1 leek (not including dark green
  portion), coarsely chopped
1 medium onion, coarsely
  chopped
1 jalapeno pepper, seeded and
  finely chopped

½ pound (227 grams)
  mushrooms of your choice,
  cut in large pieces 1 teaspoon salt
½ teaspoon white pepper
¾ teaspoon cumin
½ teaspoon sugar

Vegetables: In a baking pan that can be used on top of the stove (or a large skillet), heat oil on medium-high heat. Sauté mushrooms, leek, onion and jalapeno pepper together with seasonings until lightly caramelized, about 10 minutes. Onions should be light brown.

Sauce:	2 medium ripe tomatoes,
1/4 cup white wine	seeded and coarsely chopped
1 cup duck sauce (such as Gold's)	

Sauce: Add wine and deglaze the pan, scraping up the browned bits from the bottom of the pan with a wooden spoon. Bring to a boil and cook until 3 tablespoons of pan juices remain. Add duck sauce and tomatoes and mix thoroughly. Heat until liquid is bubbling.

Assembly: Place chicken on top of vegetables, keeping dark meat and breasts separate. Cover pan tightly and place in bottom 1/3 of oven for 25 minutes. Breasts should now be ready, so remove pan from oven. Transfer breasts to a platter and keep warm. Return pan to oven for another 20 minutes to allow dark meat to finish cooking.

Serve chicken on bed of sautéed vegetables, or strain the contents of the pan and use the remaining sauce over the chicken.

Yield: 6 servings.

Recipe by Bernie Zucker

Cooking is like love. It should be entered into with abandon or not at all.
Harriet van Horne

Chicken Chasseur

1 chicken, cut in eighths (or use skinless boneless breasts or any parts you prefer)
2 tablespoons canola oil
1 tablespoon margarine
6 ounces sliced fresh mushrooms (about 2 cups)
1/2 of a 5 1/2 ounce can (5 tablespoons) tomato paste
1 can (8 ounces/227 ml) tomato sauce
1 large onion, sliced
pinch of sugar
salt, pepper and garlic to taste
1/4 cup each chopped fresh dill and parsley
1/2 teaspoon dried chervil (or to taste)
3 to 4 ounces white wine
2 to 3 tablespoons brandy
additional chopped fresh parsley, to garnish

Preheat oven to 350°F.

Rinse chicken pieces and pat dry. Heat oil in a large skillet on medium-high heat. Add chicken pieces and brown on all sides until almost done, about 10 to 15 minutes.

Transfer chicken to a greased baking dish. (Don't bother cleaning the skillet.) Bake uncovered at 350°F for 30 minutes.

Add margarine (and a little more oil, if needed) to skillet. Sauté mushrooms and onions for 2 to 3 minutes on medium-high heat. Add tomato sauce, tomato paste and sugar. Reduce heat to medium and simmer uncovered for 5 minutes, stirring occasionally.

Add salt, pepper, garlic, dill, parsley and chervil. Stir in wine and brandy; cook until sauce is reduced and coats the spoon nicely, stirring occasionally.

Serve chicken and sauce on bed of noodles or rice. Top with sauce; garnish with chopped parsley.

Yield: 4 to 6 servings.

Recipe by Toba Weiss

Chicken on Rice

2 chickens, cut in eighths
³/₄ cup all-purpose flour,
  seasoned with salt, pepper
  and garlic powder (or
  seasoned salt)
2 tablespoons canola oil

¹/₂ cup chopped onion
¹/₂ cup chopped green pepper
¹/₂ cup sliced mushrooms
1 cup raw rice, rinsed and
  drained
3 cups chicken broth

Preheat oven to 400°F.

Rinse chicken pieces and pat dry. Lightly coat chicken pieces with seasoned flour.

Heat oil in a large skillet on medium-high heat. Brown chicken in batches on all sides until golden, about 8 to 10 minutes. Remove from skillet and set aside.

Add onion, green pepper and mushrooms to skillet and sauté 5 to 7 minutes, until golden. Combine vegetables with rice in a greased baking dish large enough to hold chicken in a single layer. Pour chicken broth over rice mixture.

Cover and bake at 400°F for 20 minutes. Arrange chicken on top, cover and bake an additional 45 to 50 minutes, until tender.

Yield: 8 servings.

Recipe by Lois Friedman Fine

Chicken Oriental

Chicken:
1 broiler, cut into 8 to 12 pieces (or use pieces of chicken breast)
½ cup all-purpose flour seasoned with salt and pepper
4 to 8 tablespoons margarine

Sauce:
4 to 8 tablespoons margarine
¼ cup honey
¼ cup lemon juice
1 tablespoon soy sauce

Preheat oven 350°F.

Chicken: Rinse chicken pieces and pat dry. Place seasoned flour in a plastic bag. Add a few chicken pieces at a time and shake well, coating chicken with flour mixture.

Melt margarine in a 9-inch x 13-inch baking pan. Place chicken pieces skin-side down in pan. Bake uncovered at 350°F for 30 minutes. While chicken is baking, make sauce.

Sauce: Melt margarine in a saucepan over low heat. Add honey, lemon juice and soy sauce; stir well to combine.

Remove chicken from oven. Turn chicken pieces over and cover with sauce. Bake uncovered 30 minutes longer, basting occasionally.

Yield: 4 to 6 servings.

Recipe by Bea Myers

Chicken With Olives, Apricots And Capers

1 cup dry vermouth
1 cup kalamata olives
1 cup dried apricots
½ cup drained capers
1 teaspoon grated orange zest
½ cup orange juice
3 tablespoons dried basil
(fresh is better)

¼ cup white wine vinegar
2 tablespoons olive oil
6 cloves garlic, minced
8 chicken legs with thighs
(separate if desired)
salt and pepper, to taste
1 cup brown sugar, packed

In a large, shallow glass bowl, combine vermouth, olives, apricots, capers, orange zest, juice, vinegar, basil, oil and garlic. Add chicken, turning to coat it on both sides. Cover and marinate in refrigerator for 12 hours.

Preheat oven to 375°F. Spray a large roasting pan or baking dish with non-stick spray.

Arrange chicken, olives, apricots, and capers in a single layer in roasting pan. Season well with salt and pepper. Pour any remaining marinade over top. Sprinkle with brown sugar.

Bake at 375°F for 1 hour or longer, basting often. Juices should run clear when chicken is pierced.

Yield: 8 servings.

Recipe by G.G.

Chinese Chicken

Marinade:
1 egg
3 tablespoons cornstarch
½ teaspoon salt
1 tablespoon grapeseed oil

Chicken and Vegetables:
2 whole chicken breasts,
skinned, boned and cut into
cubes
2 tablespoons oil (approximately)
½ to 1 tablespoon minced
fresh ginger

1 small clove garlic, minced
2 cups broccoli florets
½ of a green pepper, diced
½ of a red pepper, diced
2 cups sliced mushrooms
Optional: snow peas, sliced
carrots and/or shallots

Sauce:
1 teaspoon chili paste (or
black pepper)
3 tablespoons soy sauce
3 tablespoons orange juice
2 tablespoons sugar

Combine ingredients for marinade in a large bowl. Add chicken cubes and marinate them for at least 30 minutes (or up to 24 hours in the refrigerator).

Add oil to wok or frying pan. When hot, add chicken and stir-fry 4 to 5 minutes, until no longer pink. Remove chicken from wok.

Add more oil, if necessary. Add ginger and garlic; stir-fry for 30 seconds. Add hard vegetables first (e.g., broccoli, carrots) and stir-fry 2 to 3 minutes. Add soft veggies (e.g., peppers, mushrooms, snow peas, shallots) and stir-fry 1 minute longer, until tender-crisp.

Combine ingredients for sauce in a small bowl and mix well; add to wok. Return chicken to wok and heat through, 1 to 2 minutes longer. Serve with rice, if desired.

Yield: 4 servings.

Recipe by Ruth Garbe

Cornish Hens

2 Cornish hens, cut in half	2 shallots, minced
¼ cup flour	2 cloves garlic, minced
1 tablespoon minced fresh rosemary leaves	¾ cup dry white wine
	⅓ cup chicken stock
salt and freshly ground black pepper to taste	1 teaspoon anchovy paste
	3 sprigs rosemary
3 tablespoons olive oil	

Preheat oven to 375°F.

Rinse Cornish hens and pat dry. Combine flour, rosemary, salt and pepper in a plastic bag and mix well. Coat hens in seasoned flour; shake off excess.

Heat oil in large ovenproof skillet. Sauté hens over medium heat for 10 to 15 minutes, until golden brown, turning them over once. Remove from pan and place on a plate.

Add shallots and garlic to skillet. Cook until golden, about 2 to 3 minutes. Remove from skillet and set aside. Pour off fat and return hens to skillet.

In a bowl, whisk wine, chicken stock and anchovy paste together until smooth. Pour over hens and bring to a boil. Sprinkle with rosemary sprigs, reserved shallots and garlic.

Transfer to oven and bake, uncovered, until golden brown about 35 to 40 minutes. Serve on warm platter and top with sauce.

Yield: 2 to 4 servings.

Recipe by Mayta Markson

Dijon Chicken Breasts

3 whole chicken breasts, with skin and bone, split in half (³/₄ pound/375 grams each)
¹/₂ cup Dijon mustard (such as Maille)
5 tablespoons vegetable oil, divided use
2 to 3 green onions, minced
¹/₂ teaspoon tarragon leaves
¹/₄ teaspoon hot pepper sauce (such as Tabasco)
³/₄ cup unsalted soda cracker crumbs or breadcrumbs

Preheat oven to 375°F.

Rinse chicken pieces and pat dry. In a small bowl, mix mustard with 2 tablespoons oil, green onions, tarragon and hot pepper sauce. Mix into a paste and slather over chicken breasts.

Dip chicken breasts into crumbs, coating well. Arrange chicken in a single layer in a large greased casserole. Drizzle remaining 3 tablespoons of oil over chicken.

Bake uncovered at 375°F for 1 hour, until nicely browned. Juices should run clear when chicken is pierced with the tip of a knife.

Yield: 6 servings.

Recipe by Brooky Robins

Fragrant Chicken and Mushrooms

1 chicken (3 pounds/1.4 kg), cut in eighths	$\frac{1}{2}$ cup carrots, chopped
salt and freshly ground pepper	12 small mushrooms
3 tablespoons all-purpose flour seasoned with salt and pepper	$\frac{1}{2}$ teaspoon dried thyme
	1 bay leaf
	1-inch piece orange peel
2 tablespoons olive oil	2 cups dry red or white wine
8 cloves garlic, peeled (do not chop)	1 cup chicken stock
	1 tablespoon tomato paste
1 onion, chopped	2 tablespoons brandy
	2 tablespoons chopped parsley

Rinse chicken pieces and pat dry. Trim fat from chicken; sprinkle lightly with salt and pepper. Lightly coat chicken with seasoned flour.

Heat oil in a large skillet on medium heat. Add chicken in batches and sauté 3 to 5 minutes on each side, until golden. Remove chicken from skillet and place on a large plate.

Add garlic, onion and carrots to skillet and sauté until onions begin to turn colour, about 5 minutes. Add mushrooms and sauté for 2 to 3 minutes. Add thyme, bay leaf and orange peel. Stir in wine, chicken stock, tomato paste and brandy. Bring to a boil and cook for 3 minutes, stirring occasionally.

Return chicken to skillet. Cover and simmer gently for 25 minutes.

Remove chicken and vegetables from pan and keep warm. Raise heat to high and reduce the stock mixture until it has thickened slightly, 3 to 5 minutes. Season with salt and pepper and pour over chicken. Sprinkle with parsley.

Yield: 4 servings.

Recipe by Gloria Lepofsky

Grandma Celia's Chicken Fricassee

Prepare as much chicken as you want by cutting it into reasonable-size pieces. Remove the skin when possible. Any cuts of chicken are suitable. To reduce the cost, omit breasts.

Cut off the narrow, meatless end from the drumsticks. Cut thighs, wings and breasts (with the bone) into sections, throwing out the meatless sections.

Preheat oven to 325°F. Brown lots of chopped onions in oil in a large roasting pan or casserole on top of the stove, over medium heat.

Add chicken pieces to onions and cover with cold water. Add an ample amount of ketchup (the Heinz 57 variety) until the liquid is a good pink colour. Mix well. (Unfortunately I have no measure to tell you but you can't go wrong even if you add a little too much the first time!)

Cover the pan first with aluminum foil, then with the lid, making sure it fits tightly. It is important to cook this covered for the first 1½ hours to avoid evaporation. Remove the foil and lid to make the brown gravy richer and more concentrated. Season with salt and pepper; cook uncovered 1 hour longer.

Getting the gravy right and not overcooking the chicken (which then falls off the bone) is a matter of trial and error. Keeping an eye on it and stirring will help. Serve on rice, kasha or farfel. This makes a great meal on a cold winter night.

Yield: It depends on how much chicken you started out with!

Recipe by Joni Seligman

Honey Basil Chicken

4 skinless, boneless single
chicken breasts
(1 pound/500 grams)
Marinade:
1 cup raspberry vinegar
2 tablespoons low-sodium soy
sauce

3 tablespoons Dijon mustard
2 tablespoons honey
2 tablespoons minced fresh
basil
pinch of black pepper
$\frac{1}{2}$ teaspoon dried thyme

Rinse chicken breasts and pat dry. Combine marinade ingredients in a large bowl. Add chicken, cover and refrigerate for 15 minutes.

Spray cold grill with 100 percent vegetable oil or non-stick spray. Heat coals until very hot and then spray grill again just before adding chicken.

Remove chicken from marinade; reserve marinade. Grill chicken breasts for 5 to 6 minutes per side.

Place reserved marinade in a small saucepan and bring to a boil. Simmer for 5 minutes or until reduced by half. To serve, pour hot marinade over chicken.

Yield: 4 servings.

Recipe by Ricky Zabitsky

Marinated Basil Chicken

6 chicken thighs
6 chicken drumsticks
½ cup olive oil
½ cup freshly squeezed lemon
  juice
5 cloves garlic, crushed

1 large bunch fresh basil
  (about 50 leaves, washed
  and chopped)
1 teaspoon salt
coarse black pepper, to taste

Preheat oven to 350°F.

Rinse chicken pieces and pat dry. Combine oil, lemon juice, garlic and basil in a large mixing bowl (a roasting pan also works well); mix well. Dip chicken pieces in sauce, coating them well on all sides, as well as under the skin.

Arrange chicken pieces in a single layer on a large parchment-lined baking pan. Pour remaining sauce over chicken. Sprinkle with salt and pepper.

Bake uncovered at 350°F for 50 to 60 minutes, basting occasionally, until chicken is nicely browned.

Yield: 6 servings. Freezes well.

Recipe by Margalit Glazer

Moroccan Chicken with Couscous and Zucchini Pilaf

Spice Mixture/Chicken:
1 tsp. orange juice
2 tablespoons olive oil
1 tablespoon honey
³/₄ teaspoon ground cumin
³/₄ teaspoon ground coriander
1/4 teaspoon salt
¹/₄ teaspoon pepper
¹/₂ teaspoon each cinnamon,
   paprika and dried mint
4 boneless, skinless single
   chicken breasts

Couscous Pilaf:
1 tablespoon olive oil
2 cloves garlic, minced
1 small onion, chopped
¹/₂ teaspoon salt
¹/₄ teaspoon pepper
1 cup water
¹/₂ cup orange juice
¹/₄ cup diced dried apricots
1 cup couscous
1 zucchini, shredded

In a small bowl, prepare spice mixture by whisking together the orange juice, oil, honey, cumin, coriander, salt, pepper, cinnamon, paprika and mint.

Preheat broiler. Place chicken on a broiler pan or foil-lined rimmed baking sheet. Brush chicken with half of spice mixture.

Broil chicken for 8 to 10 minutes. Turn chicken pieces over and brush with remaining spice mixture. Broil 8 to 10 minutes longer, or until chicken is no longer pink inside and juices run clear.

Meanwhile, prepare couscous. In a saucepan, heat oil over medium heat. Add garlic, onion, salt and pepper. Cook for 5 minutes, until softened. Add water, orange juice and apricots; bring to a boil. Stir in couscous and zucchini. Cover and remove from heat. Let stand for 5 minutes. Fluff with a fork and serve with the chicken.

Yield: 4 servings.

Recipe by Dr. Ricky Pasternak

Myra's Red Currant Jelly Chicken

2 small fryers, cut up	Sauce:
¾ cup all-purpose flour seasoned with salt and pepper	¼ cup orange juice
	¾ cup red currant jelly, melted
¼ cup canola or grapeseed oil	1 teaspoon dry mustard
1 large onion, thinly sliced	1 teaspoon powdered ginger
salt & pepper to taste	

Preheat oven to 350°F.

Rinse chicken pieces and pat dry. Lightly coat chicken with seasoned flour, shaking off excess.

Heat oil on medium high heat in a large ovenproof skillet. Add onion and sauté for 5 minutes, until golden. Add chicken pieces and brown them lightly on all sides. Transfer the skillet to oven and bake uncovered for ½ hour at 350°F.

Combine ingredients for sauce in a bowl; mix well. Pour sauce mixture over chicken. Bake uncovered ½ hour longer, basting occasionally. If chicken gets too brown, cover it loosely with aluminum foil.

Yield: 6 to 8 servings.

Note: This tastes even better if made the day before. Reheat at 325°F for 20 minutes.

Recipe by Myra Cohen

Orange Baked Chicken

3 whole chickens, cut into
  eighths
3 cups cornflakes, crushed
Kosher salt, pepper and garlic
  powder, to taste
¼ pound (½ cup) margarine,
  melted

Sauce:
1 can (12 ounces/355 ml)
  frozen orange juice
  concentrate, thawed
juice of 1 lemon
2 heaping tablespoons orange
  marmalade
2 teaspoons crystallized
  ginger, cut in small pieces
1 tablespoon sherry
½ cup slivered almonds

Preheat oven to 375°F.

Rinse chicken pieces and pat dry. Combine cornflakes with salt, pepper and garlic powder; mix well. Dip chicken pieces first in melted margarine, then in cornflakes, coating them well.

Arrange chicken in a single layer on parchment-lined baking sheet(s). Bake uncovered at 375°F for 1 hour, until golden brown.

Combine ingredients for sauce in a saucepan and mix well. Bring to a boil, reduce heat and simmer uncovered for 10 minutes, stirring occasionally. Pour over chicken.

Yield: 12 servings.

Recipe by Phyllis Crystal

SALADS AND DRESSINGS

Belgian Endive
with Creamy Mustard Dressing

2 Belgian endives
1 small head Boston lettuce
½ cup walnuts (large pieces),
   lightly toasted, to garnish

Creamy Mustard Dressing:
2 tablespoons lemon juice
1 teaspoon salt
¼ teaspoon black pepper
1 tablespoon Dijon mustard
1 small clove garlic, finely
   minced
⅓ cup olive oil
1 tablespoon chopped fresh
   tarragon

Separate leaves from endives and lettuce. Wash thoroughly and dry well. Break lettuce into pieces about the same size as endives; place greens in a large bowl.

Dressing: In a small bowl, whisk lemon juice with salt, pepper, mustard and garlic. Whisk in oil and tarragon.

Just before serving, combine greens with dressing and sprinkle with walnuts.

Yield: 4 servings.

Tip: I use either lemon juice or red wine vinegar in this salad.

Recipe by G.G.

Black Bean Salad

2 pounds (1 kg) dried black beans
1 jalapeno pepper, seeded and minced
2 red onions, coarsely chopped
1 bunch fresh cilantro/coriander, stems and leaves coarsely chopped
1½ tablespoons salt
1 tablespoon pepper

Place beans in a pot and cover with cold water. Bring to a boil, reduce heat and simmer until al dente, about 40 to 45 minutes. Do not overcook. Drain and cool.

Transfer drained beans to a large bowl. Add jalapeno pepper, onions, cilantro, salt and pepper.

Dressing:
1 tablespoon ground cumin
2 garlic cloves, minced
½ cup red wine vinegar
1 cup olive oil

Combine ingredients for dressing in a jar and shake to blend. Pour over bean mixture and mix well. Refrigerate for several hours before serving.

Yield: 12 to 16 servings.

Note: If desired, soak black beans in triple the amount of water overnight. Drain and rinse well. Soaking them makes them easier to digest.

Recipe by Mayta Markson

Marinated Broccoli Salad

3 bunches or more of broccoli (use only the florets), cooked	1 or 2 peppers (red or yellow), diced
2 medium red onions, thinly sliced	1 can (19 ounces/540 ml) chick peas, drained and rinsed

Combine broccoli florets, onions, peppers and chick peas in a large bowl. Mix well.

Marinade:	⅓ cup sugar
½ cup olive oil (garlic-flavoured)	1 tsp. Worcestershire sauce dried parsley flakes or minced
¾ cup vinegar	fresh basil

Mix together olive oil, vinegar and sugar in a small bowl. Blend in Worcestershire sauce.

Add marinade to broccoli mixture; sprinkle with parsley or basil. Cover and refrigerate for several hours to blend flavours.

Yield: 10 to 12 servings.

Recipe by Myra Cohen

Cabbage Salad

2 packages chicken-flavoured
Ramen noodles
1 bag shredded cabbage

1 cup toasted sliced almonds
¼ cup toasted sesame seeds
6 scallions, minced

Remove seasoning packets from Ramen noodles and reserve. They will be used in the dressing. Combine noodles with cabbage, almonds, sesame seeds and scallions in a large bowl. Mix well.

Dressing:
¾ cup vegetable oil
6 tablespoons cider vinegar

2 packages Ramen noodle
seasoning
½ cup sugar

Combine dressing ingredients in a glass jar and shake well. This can be done earlier in the day. Add dressing to cabbage mixture just before serving. Toss well.

Yield: 6 to 8 servings.

Recipe by Marilyn Himmel

Coleslaw

1 medium cabbage, finely shredded

10 medium carrots, peeled and finely shredded

1 green pepper, seeded and finely chopped

1 small onion, grated

Combine cabbage, carrots, green pepper and onion in a large bowl. Mix well.

Dressing:
$^3/_4$ cup mayonnaise
$^1/_4$ cup white vinegar

$^1/_4$ cup granulated sugar (or more to taste)
2 teaspoons salt
black pepper, to taste

Combine dressing ingredients in a bowl and blend thoroughly. Add to cabbage mixture and mix well. Adjust seasonings to taste. Cover and refrigerate for 3 to 4 hours before serving to blend flavours.

Alternative Dressing:
1 cup white vinegar
$^1/_3$ cup salad oil

$^1/_2$ cup granulated sugar
salt and pepper, to taste

Combine all ingredients and mix well. Use instead of mayonnaise dressing.

Yield: 12 to 15 servings.

Recipe by Pauline Toker

Caesar Salad

1 small head romaine lettuce
2 cloves garlic
4 anchovy fillets
$^1/_4$ teaspoon plus 4 tablespoons red wine vinegar
$^1/_2$ teaspoon dry mustard
$^1/_3$ cup olive oil
$^1/_2$ teaspoon drained bottled horseradish

$1^1/_2$ tablespoons fresh lemon juice
soft-boiled egg (cooked 1 minute)
2 tablespoons freshly grated Parmesan cheese
3 tablespoons croutons
freshly ground pepper, to taste

Wash lettuce well; spin dry and tear into bite-size pieces.

In a large bowl, smash together garlic and anchovy fillets with $^1/_4$ teaspoon of vinegar. Whisk in mustard, remaining $^1/_4$ cup vinegar, oil, horseradish, lemon juice and egg. Whisk the dressing until well blended.

Add lettuce and toss lightly. Sprinkle salad with Parmesan cheese, croutons and pepper.

Yield: 2 to 3 servings.

Recipe by G.G.

Cape Cod Salad

2 heads Boston lettuce
4 hearts of palm, sliced
1½ pounds (750 grams) green
    beans, blanched in salted
    boiling water
juice of ½ lemon

2 cloves garlic, crushed
1 red onion, finely sliced
    (optional)
1 pint red cherry or grape
    tomatoes
3 sprigs chopped fresh basil

Wash lettuce and dry it well. Tear into bite-size pieces and place in a large salad bowl. Add hearts of palm.

Drain beans; drizzle lemon juice over warm beans. Add to salad bowl along with garlic, onion, tomatoes, and basil. Toss vegetables with vinaigrette dressing.

Vinaigrette Dressing:
⅔ cup extra-virgin olive oil
⅓ cup red wine vinegar

1 tablespoon Dijon mustard
1 tablespoon sugar

Combine all ingredients for dressing in a jar and shake well.

Yield: 6 to 8 servings.

Recipe by G.G.

Chick Pea Salad

1 can (19 ounces/540 ml)
  chickpeas, drained
2 tablespoons chopped green
  or red onions
1 tomato, diced (optional)

2 cloves garlic, minced
$\frac{1}{2}$ cup chopped fresh parsley
$\frac{1}{4}$ cup olive oil
1 tablespoon lemon juice
salt and pepper, to taste

In a large bowl, combine all ingredients and toss well. Chill for 2 hours

Serve with Aïoli. (See page 16)

Yield: 4 servings. This also makes a delicious appetizer.

Recipe by G.G.

*Food is an extension of creativity and
love. When we cook for someone in need
it is always a heroic deed.*

G.G.

Grapefruit-Avocado Salad
with Honey Dressing

Dressing:
¼ cup olive oil
2 tablespoons tarragon vinegar
   or white wine vinegar
1 tablespoon liquid honey
¼ tsp salt

Salad:
4 pink grapefruit
2 ripe avocados, preferably
   Hass
4 small Belgian endives

Dressing: Whisk oil together with vinegar, honey and salt in a small bowl. Set aside.

Salad: Peel grapefruit. Remove all of the white pith and cut between membranes to make grapefruit wedges. Cut avocados in half; remove pits. Peel avocados and cut into thin long slices. Trim ends from endive and separate leaves. Now you have the makings of an aesthetic salad.

Decorate individual serving plates or a large platter, alternating grapefruit sections with avocado slices and arranging them attractively on top of endive leaves. Drizzle with dressing.

Yield: 6 servings.

To prepare ingredients for this salad in advance: Prepare dressing and leave it at room temperature. Cut grapefruit into segments, seal them in a plastic bag and refrigerate. Cover endive leaves with a damp paper towel for up to a day in the refrigerator. Slice avocado just before arranging. It discolours if slice too early.

Recipe by G.G.

Green Beans - Lemon Mustard Vinaigrette

1 pound (500 grams) green
beans, tipped and tailed
2 teaspoons Dijon mustard
2 teaspoons freshly squeezed
lemon juice

6 tablespoons extra-virgin
olive oil
1 shallot or 1 clove garlic,
minced
10 cherry tomatoes, halved, to
garnish

Bring a pot of water to boil. Drop beans into boiling water and cook for 4 to 7 minutes, depending on texture you desire. Meanwhile, make vinaigrette.

In a small bowl, whisk together mustard and lemon juice. Slowly add olive oil, 1 tablespoon at a time and whisk together. Add shallot or garlic

When beans are done, drain them and immediately drop them into a bowl of ice water. This will keep them bright green. Drain well.

Toss drained beans with dressing. Use only as much salad dressing as you deem necessary, retaining the rest for salads or sandwiches. Garnish with cherry tomatoes. Serve at room temperature or chilled.

Yield: 4 servings.

Tip: This can be prepared ahead of time.

Recipe by G.G.

Green Salad

½ cup blanched slivered almonds	1 cup chopped celery
3 tablespoons white sugar	2 green onions, chopped
1 head Boston lettuce	1½ cups orange segments
½ head romaine lettuce	(2 oranges)

In a small pan over medium heat, cook almonds together with sugar, stirring constantly, until almonds are roasted and sugar has dissolved. (Watch carefully as the nuts brown easily.) Let cool. Store in an airtight container.

Combine romaine and Boston lettuces together in a large bowl. Add celery, green onions and orange segments. At serving time, drizzle with dressing and toss lightly.

Dressing:	¼ cup vegetable oil
½ teaspoon salt	1 tablespoon white sugar
dash of pepper	2 tablespoons white vinegar
1 tablespoon chopped fresh parsley	dash of Tabasco sauce

Mix dressing ingredients together in a small bowl. Can be prepared in advance and refrigerated.

Yield: 4 to 6 servings.

Recipe by Ronda Roth

Red Potato Salad

Ellie's favourite. So simple, simply delicious!

2 pounds (1 kg) red potatoes, cubed (do not peel)
⅓ cup diced red or Spanish onion
2 tablespoons Dijon mustard
2 to 3 tablespoons whole-grain mustard
¼ cup olive oil
½ teaspoon salt
freshly ground black pepper

Boil potatoes in salted water to cover for 8 to 10 minutes, or until tender. Drain well.

Place potatoes in a large bowl. Add onion, mustards, olive oil, salt and pepper to potatoes while they are still warm. Mix well.

Cover and refrigerate for several hours or overnight. Bring to room temperature before serving.

Yield: 4 to 6 servings.

Recipe by G.G.

Oriental Chicken Salad

2 whole skinless, boneless
  chicken breasts, halved
1 can (or ½ package) Chinese
  noodles
1 package (about 2 cups)
  fresh bean sprouts
1 cup snow peas, cut on the
  diagonal into thirds
1 cup frozen peas, thawed
1 cup sliced celery or fennel
1 cup sliced red peppers
1 cup sliced carrots and/or
  broccoli (or any other
  vegetables you have on hand)
toasted sesame seeds,
  to garnish

Sauce:
⅓ cup soy sauce
2 tablespoons Oriental sesame
  oil
2 tablespoons salad oil
1 tablespoon sugar or honey
2 tablespoons orange juice
1 tablespoon grated orange
  zest
salt and pepper, to taste
1 clove garlic, minced

Poach chicken breasts in simmering water to cover until tender, about 15 minutes. Let cool. Cut into bite-size pieces.

When ready to serve, layer ingredients on a shallow serving platter in the following order: Chinese noodles, bean sprouts, snow peas, peas, celery or fennel, red peppers, carrots and/or broccoli. Top with chicken pieces; sprinkle with sesame seeds.

Sauce: Combine all ingredients for sauce and mix well. Drizzle over salad and serve immediately.

Yield: 4 servings. This recipe can be doubled easily.

Recipe by Anne Estern

Roast Chicken & Apricot Salad

1 package (10 ounces/300 grams) baby spinach leaves, washed and dried
4 roasted boneless chicken breasts, thinly sliced
2 orange peppers, sliced

12 dried apricots
6 fresh apricots
⅓ cup pine nuts, toasted
1 recipe Apricot Dressing (below)

Arrange salad ingredients attractively on a platter or individual plates. Drizzle with dressing. Serve immediately.

Apricot Dressing:
½ cup balsamic vinegar
⅔ cup olive oil
½ teaspoon minced garlic

¼ cup apricot jam, liquified (microwave until fluid)
2 teaspoons chopped fresh parsley
fresh black pepper, to taste

In a small bowl, stir together all ingredients until blended.

Yield: 4 servings.

Recipe by G.G.

Salad Exotica

Salad:
1 bunch fresh spinach, washed and dried
1 head romaine lettuce, washed and dried
4 mandarin oranges, in segments (or 2 – 10 ounce cans, well-drained)
1 Spanish onion (or other sweet onion), thinly sliced
1 red pepper, thinly sliced
1 orange pepper, thinly sliced
2 cups sliced mushrooms
2 large avocados, pitted, peeled and sliced (add at the last moment)

2 cups bean sprouts
2 to 3 tablespoons minced fresh dill
toasted pine nuts, to garnish

Dressing:
12 tablespoons olive oil
4 tablespoons white wine vinegar
1 teaspoon mustard powder
$1/4$ teaspoon sugar
3 or 4 cloves garlic, minced
fresh dill to taste, chopped finely
salt to taste

Combine salad ingredients in a large bowl. It is best to add the avocados just before serving to prevent them from discolouring.

In a small bowl, combine ingredients for dressing and blend well. Drizzle over salad at serving time and toss well.

Yield: 8 servings.

Recipe by G.G.

Tomato and Mozzarella Platter

lettuce leaves, for lining
serving platter
8 ripe, firm tomatoes, sliced
crosswise ¼-inch thick
2 red onions (same size as
tomatoes), thinly sliced
crosswise

1 pound (500 grams) fresh
buffalo mozzarella, sliced
1 bunch fresh basil leaves, for
garnish

Cover a round platter with lettuce leaves. Overlap alternating slices of tomatoes, onions and cheese. You can prepare this in advance, cover the platter with plastic wrap and refrigerate it for several hours.

Before serving, drizzle desired amount of vinaigrette over salad. Garnish with basil leaves.

Yield: 8 to 10 servings.

Vinaigrette:
4 tablespoons balsamic
vinegar
1 teaspoon Dijon mustard
½ teaspoon salt

½ teaspoon freshly ground
pepper
¾ cup extra-virgin olive oil
2 tablespoons basil, chopped

Combine vinegar, mustard, salt and pepper in a small bowl. Whisk until completely blended. Slowly add oil in a steady stream, whisking continually. Stir in basil. Taste for seasoning. Refrigerate vinaigrette for up to 1 week. Remove from refrigerator 1 hour before serving and whisk thoroughly to make sure dressing is emulsified.

Yield: 1 cup.

Recipe by G.G.

Tuscan Tuna Salad Nicoise

Salad:
1 medium head romaine lettuce, torn into bite-size pieces
3 handfuls green lettuce leaves
10 large black pitted olives
½ package goat cheese, crumbled
2 cans (6 ounces/175 grams each) water-packed solid white tuna, drained
2 roasted red peppers (from a jar), drained, cut in julienne strips
1 jar (6 ounces/175 grams) marinated artichoke hearts, drained
3 hard boiled eggs, quartered
4 medium red potatoes, boiled and chilled
½ jar of capers

In a large serving bowl, lightly toss the above salad ingredients together. Cover and chill until serving time.

Dressing:
2 tablespoons balsamic vinegar
2 tablespoons red wine vinegar
2 tablespoons water
½ teaspoon granulated sugar
¼ teaspoon each salt and freshly ground pepper (or lemon pepper)
2 tablespoons chopped fresh parsley
1 tablespoon canola oil
1 tablespoon olive oil

Combine ingredients for dressing in a bottle. Shake together vigorously to blend; drizzle over salad. Toss lightly and serve chilled.

Yield: 6 servings.

Recipe by G.G.

Wild Rice Grape Salad

5 cups water
¾ cup wild rice
1 teaspoon salt
⅛ teaspoon grated nutmeg
1½ cups long-grain rice
6 green onions, thinly sliced
2 cups seedless green grapes, halved
¼ cup extra-virgin olive oil
2 tablespoons toasted sesame oil

3 tablespoons freshly squeezed lemon or lime juice
1 tablespoon Dijon mustard
2 tablespoons honey
1 tablespoon minced fresh ginger (or to taste)
½ cup fresh basil, plus additional for garnishing

In a large wide pot, combine water, wild rice, salt and nutmeg. Cover and bring to a boil. Reduce heat to low and simmer for 40 minutes.

Stir in long-grain rice. Cover and continue simmering 20 to 25 minutes longer. Transfer to a large bowl and cool slightly. Stir green onions and grapes into rice.

In a small bowl, whisk together olive oil, sesame oil, lemon or lime juice, mustard and honey. Add ginger. Stir into rice mixture to evenly coat.

Cover and set aside for at least 1 to 3 hours to blend flavours (or refrigerate for up to one day).

Add basil just before serving (it darkens quickly). Serve with additional basil leaves for decoration.

Yield: 8 servings.

Tip: This salad is so pretty and it can be made a day ahead. It only takes 15 minutes to assemble once all the ingredients are prepared. Total cooking time for rice is 1 hour.

Recipe by G.G.

Excellent Garlic Dressing

½ cup extra-virgin olive oil
1 garlic clove, crushed
1 hard-cooked egg, finely
    grated
1 teaspoon mayonnaise

drops of Worcestershire sauce
grated Swiss cheese, to taste
salt and pepper, to taste
juice of ½ small lemon

Combine all ingredients and blend well.

Yield: about 1 cup.

Recipe by G.G.

Gloria's Balsamic Vinaigrette

1 small shallot
1 clove garlic
2 tablespoons fresh parsley
1/2 cup garlic-flavoured olive
  oil
1 teaspoon herb mixture
(your favourite)

3 tablespoons balsamic
  vinegar
3 teaspoons honey mustard
freshly ground black pepper,
  to taste

Combine all ingredients except black pepper in a food processor and process until smooth. Add a few grindings of pepper. Toss lightly with your favourite greens.

Yield: makes about 3/4 cup.

Tip: This dressing can be prepared several hours ahead.

Recipe by G.G.

Pear Leek Dressing for Green Salad

1 tablespoon olive oil	⅓ cup white wine vinegar
½ of a Bosc pear, sliced or chopped	⅓ cup additional olive oil
1 cup leeks (white part only), chopped	¼ cup pear or apple juice
freshly ground black pepper, to taste	½ clove garlic, minced
	1 teaspoon sugar
	2 teaspoons chopped chives

In a pan, heat 1 tablespoon of oil on medium heat. Add pear, leeks and pepper; sauté together until pear and leeks have softened, about 15 minutes.

Pour pear/leek mixture into food processor. Add remaining ingredients except chives; process until smooth. Stir in chives.

Yield: about 1 cup dressing.

Recipe by G.G.

Oakdale Salad

Raspberry Dressing:

2 tablespoons frozen raspberry purée

6 tablespoons raspberry vinegar

pinch of salt and pepper

1 teaspoon Worcestershire sauce

1 shallot, finely chopped

1 clove garlic, puréed

1 teaspoon Dijon mustard

$\frac{1}{8}$ cup olive oil

$\frac{1}{4}$ cup canola oil

Raspberry Dressing: Combine all ingredients except olive and canola oils in a bowl; mix well. Slowly whisk in oils until blended. Strain dressing before using. You should have about 1 cup dressing.

$\frac{1}{2}$ cup olive oil

Juice of 2 lemons

4 whole cloves

1 sprig rosemary

2 cloves garlic, puréed

4 single boneless, skinless chicken breasts

1 pound California mix greens

1 ounce alfalfa sprouts

8 ounces toffee almonds

2 ounces Danish blue cheese, crumbled

4 ounces chopped apple

1 cup Raspberry Dressing (above)

salt and pepper

Combine olive oil, lemon juice, cloves, rosemary and garlic in a shallow bowl and blend well. Add chicken breasts and coat on both sides with marinade. Cover and refrigerate for 24 hours. Preheat oven to 375°F. Remove chicken from marinade and place on a greased baking sheet. Discard marinade. Bake chicken uncovered at 375°F for 15 minutes, or until juices run clear when pierced with the tip of a knife.

Assembly: In a large bowl, toss greens with alfalfa sprouts, almonds, cheese and apple. Arrange salad on four plates. Slice each chicken breast across the grain and place on top of salad. Drizzle with Raspberry Dressing and season with a pinch of salt and pepper.

Yield: 4 servings.

Recipe by James Saunders, Chef

Salad Dressing

2 tablespoons balsamic vinegar	1 tablespoon brown sugar
4 tablespoons olive oil	2 tablespoons orange juice
1 tablespoon mayonnaise	2 tablespoons honey mustard
	1 tablespoon anchovy paste

Combine all ingredients in a bowl and blend well. This dressing will keep for 3 weeks in refrigerator in a tightly closed container.

Yield: about ³/₄ cup dressing.

Note: This makes a delicious dressing for a green salad tossed with chopped pear, dried cranberries and feta cheese, to taste.

Recipe by Nicky Wernick

Salad Dressing Tips:

- An emulsion is always needed to bind two liquids that want to separate. Prepared mustard or fresh minced garlic will usually do the job.
- Herbs and spices can be added to boost the flavour.

Here are a few tricks to help cut the fat:
- Use two parts oil (or less) to one part vinegar.
- If you like, add wine, broth or juice to stretch the dressing. Just before serving, add an ice cube to the dressing and shake well, then remove the ice cube. (This thickens the oil and makes the dressing less watery.)
- Add just enough dressing to coat the vegetables lightly. Don't drown it!

VEGETABLES AND SIDE DISHES

Asparagus, Asparagus

Asparagus in Oven (My favourite!) Preheat oven to 500°F. Quickly rinse asparagus and trim off ends from 1 pound of asparagus. Place in pan; sprinkle with 2 tablespoons olive oil and 3 to 4 crushed garlic cloves. Roast uncovered for exactly 7 minutes. Immediately immerse asparagus in cold water for a few seconds to retain its bright green colour. Sprinkle with freshly squeezed lemon juice. Serve warm, cold or at room temperature. Serves 4.

Asparagus Sauté Parmesan Slice 1 pound asparagus into 2-inch pieces. Sauté in 2 teaspoons grapeseed oil until tender-crisp, about 3 to 4 minutes. Toss with 2 tablespoons grated Parmesan cheese. Drain and serve with lemon. Serves 2 to 4.

Asparagus Vinaigrette Boil 1 pound asparagus, covered, for about 4 minutes. Combine 1 tablespoon of grapeseed oil with 1 teaspoon Dijon mustard and 1 teaspoon red wine vinegar; mix well. Toss with drained asparagus and serve warm. Serves 2 to 4.

Asparagus with Onions and Olives Whisk together ¼ cup olive oil, 1½ tablespoons lemon juice and a pinch of salt and pepper. Add 2 heaping tablespoons of chopped red onion and ¼ cup slivered black olives. Drizzle over 1 pound of cooked hot or chilled asparagus. Serves 2 to 4.

Boiled Asparagus Boil 1 pound asparagus, covered, for 4 minutes. Whisk ¼ cup olive or grapeseed oil with 2 tablespoon lemon juice, 3 tablespoons finely chopped shallots, 1 teaspoon chopped fresh tarragon, ¼ teaspoon salt and a pinch of pepper. Toss with drained asparagus. Do not prepare more than an hour in advance. Serves 4.

Microwaved Asparagus Put 1 finely chopped onion and 2 tablespoons olive oil in a microwave-safe dish. Cover and microwave on high for 2 minutes. Stir in 2 cups asparagus, cut in 1-inch pieces. Cook covered for 2 minutes. Stir in 1 teaspoon Dijon mustard. Let stand covered for 3 minutes. Serves 2.

Recipes by G.G.

Asparagus Tempura

1½ cups cornstarch
¾ cup all-purpose flour
1 teaspoon baking powder
1 teaspoon salt
1¾ cups ice cold soda water

1 pound (500 grams)
 asparagus
4 cups vegetable oil, for
 deep-frying

Combine cornstarch with flour, baking powder and salt in a large wide bowl. Whisk in soda water until batter is consistency of thin pancake batter.

Wash asparagus well and pat very dry with paper towels.

Pour oil into a wok or large pot and heat to 375°F.

Place 6 pieces of asparagus at a time in batter to coat. Using tongs, remove each piece and place gently in hot oil. Asparagus should crisp and lightly browned in 2 to 3 minutes. Remove from oil and drain on paper towels. Repeat with remaining asparagus, working in batches of 6 pieces at a time.

Yield: 4 to 6 servings.

Tip: Cornstarch makes the coating extra-crispy. Use soy sauce or mayonnaise that has been flavoured with a little lemon juice for dipping.

Recipe by G.G.

Marinated Asparagus

2 to 3 bunches fresh asparagus	dash of pepper
	$\frac{1}{2}$ cup oil
	3 tablespoons wine vinegar
Marinade:	2 tablespoons minced fresh
2 tablespoons Dijon mustard	parsley
$\frac{1}{2}$ tsp. sugar	1 tablespoon grated onion

Steam asparagus about 4 to 6 minutes, until tender-crisp; pat dry with paper towelling.

Whisk together ingredients for marinade. Drizzle over asparagus. Can be made well ahead.

Yield: 6 to 8 servings.

Recipe by Myra Cohen

White Asparagus with Truffle Vinaigrette

1 ½ tablespoons sherry vinegar
1 ½ teaspoons fresh lemon
juice
1 bottled black truffle (15
grams, about 1 inch in
diameter), finely minced
½ tsp. Kosher salt, plus
additional for sprinkling
pepper, to taste

4 ½ tablespoons hazelnut or
walnut oil
1 ½ tablespoons chicken broth
1 ½ pounds (750 grams) white
asparagus, peeled (you may
use green asparagus)
chopped fresh chives, to
garnish

In a bowl, whisk together vinegar, lemon juice, minced truffle, ½ teaspoon kosher salt and pepper. Add oil in a slow stream, whisking constantly. Whisk in broth. Season with more salt and pepper if necessary.

Arrange asparagus on a steamer rack and sprinkle with kosher salt to taste. Cover and steam asparagus over boiling water until tender, about 10 minutes for white (or 4 to 6 minutes for green).

Transfer asparagus with tongs to paper towels and pat dry. Divide among 4 plates.

Spoon vinaigrette over asparagus and serve warm. Garnish with chopped fresh chives.

Yield: 6 servings.

Recipe by Ricky Zabitsky

Lemon Sesame Dressing (for Asparagus)

This dressing is delicious drizzled over cooked asparagus.

¼ cup butter or margarine
grated zest and juice of ½
  lemon
1 tablespoon toasted sesame
  seeds

1 teaspoon sugar
salt and pepper, to taste
¼ teaspoon garlic powder
2 bunches cooked fresh
  asparagus

Melt butter in a small saucepan. Add lemon zest, juice, sesame seeds, salt, pepper, sugar and garlic powder. Stir and heat until piping hot. Drizzle over hot cooked asparagus.

Yield: 6 to 8 servings.

Recipe by G.G.

Steamed Beets with Chives, Walnut Oil and Fresh Feta

1 bunch beets (about 1 pound/500 grams), greens removed	1 bunch chives, minced
	2 tablespoons walnut oil
	coarse salt, to taste
¼ cup fresh feta cheese	

Peel beets (rubber gloves will prevent your hands from becoming stained from the beet juices).

Place the beets in a perforated steamer pan and place another pan underneath the beets to catch their juices. Set to cook. Set timer to 30 minutes. Press start. Steam the beets until fork tender. (They may take more time if they are large.)

Use a mandoline or vegetable peeler to slice them paper-thin. Place in overlapping layers on a round plate.

Sprinkle with feta cheese, then with chives, and finally with oil. Sprinkle with coarse salt.

Yield: 4 servings.

Tip: Try to choose beets that are similar in size so they will all cook at the same time.

Recipe by James Saunders

Butternut Squash au Gratin

3½ pounds (1.5 kg) butternut squash, peeled and cut in ¾-inch cubes
⅓ cup all-purpose flour
8 ounces medium-soft goat cheese, grated (about 2 cups)

2 large leeks, white parts only, chopped
2 cups 2% milk or lactaid
1 teaspoon salt
¼ teaspoon ground nutmeg
¼ teaspoon ground ginger
½ teaspoon white pepper

Preheat over to 350°F. Butter a 2½-quart shallow baking dish (I like to use Earth Balance buttery spread).

In a large bowl, toss squash with flour until lightly coated. Place half the squash in the prepared dish. Sprinkle with leeks and half the cheese. Top with remaining squash and cheese.

In the same bowl, using any remaining flour from coating the squash, stir in milk, salt, nutmeg, ginger, and pepper; mix until blended. Pour over squash. (This can be prepared in advance and refrigerated for 2 days.)

Bake uncovered at 350°F for 1 hour, until squash is tender and sauce is thick and bubbly. Let stand 10 minutes before serving.

Yield: 12 servings.

Tips: This tastes just as delicious with lactaid milk.

Recipe by G.G.

Carrot Soufflé

Gloria's delight of a vegetable!

2 pounds carrots, peeled and sliced into coins	3 eggs
boiling water	$\frac{1}{2}$ cup brown sugar (scant)
$\frac{1}{2}$ cup butter, margarine or Earth Balance buttery spread	$1\frac{1}{2}$ teaspoons baking powder
	$\frac{3}{4}$ teaspoon baking soda

Preheat oven to 350°F. Grease a $1\frac{1}{2}$-quart soufflé dish.

In a medium saucepan, boil carrots in water until tender, about 10 to 15 minutes. Drain well.

Place carrots in a food processor and process for 20 to 30 seconds, using quick on/offs, until smooth. Add remaining ingredients and process 15 seconds longer, until blended.

Pour carrot mixture into prepared soufflé dish; spread evenly. Place the soufflé dish in a pan containing 1 inch of water. Bake uncovered at 350°F for 1 hour, until puffed and golden.

Yield: 6 to 8 servings.

Tip: If you want to make this in advance, prepare as directed above, omitting the baking powder and baking soda. Stir them in just before baking.

Recipe by G.G.

Szechuan Eggplant

1 large eggplant (do not peel)	1 tablespoon red wine vinegar
2 green onions	1½ teaspoons sugar
1 tablespoon minced garlic	1 tablespoon or more sherry
2 teaspoons minced ginger	(optional)
¼ to ½ teaspoon ground hot	2 to 3 tablespoons vegetable
chili peppers (or to taste)	oil
1 cup chicken stock	1 teaspoon Oriental sesame oil
1 tablespoon soy sauce	

Cut eggplant lengthwise into ½-inch slices, then into long strips. Set aside.

Cut green onions into 2 inch pieces and combine with garlic, ginger and hot peppers in a large bowl

Mix chicken stock, soy sauce, vinegar, sugar and sherry together in another bowl.

Heat 1 to 2 tablespoons oil in a wok or heavy skillet on high heat. Add half the eggplant and stir-fry for 4 minutes. Place on paper towels to drain. Repeat with remaining eggplant.

Heat 1 tablespoon of oil in wok. Add onion-garlic mixture and cook 30 seconds. Return eggplant to wok along with broth mixture. Bring to a boil and simmer until liquid has reduced. Stir in sesame oil. Serve on a bed of basmati rice.

Yield: 4 servings.

Note: This is delicious served with a salad made with raw mung bean sprouts, snow peas and tomatoes.

Recipe by Joni Seligman

Olives And Mushrooms In Tomato Sauce

1 can (10 ounces/300 grams) pitted green olives, drained
1 can (10 ounces/300 grams) whole mushrooms, drained
2 to 3 teaspoons canola oil
1 small onion, chopped
5 cloves garlic, crushed
1 tomato, peeled and finely diced

1 heaping tablespoon tomato paste (approximately)
1 cup water
1/4 teaspoon salt
1/4 teaspoon sugar
1 teaspoon sweet paprika
1/2 teaspoon hot paprika (optional)
1/2 teaspoon turmeric
1 cup water

Place olives in a large strainer or colander and rinse well. Add mushrooms to strainer and rinse well. Leave olives and mushrooms in the strainer to drain.

Heat oil in a large skillet on medium heat. Add onion and garlic and sauté for 5 to 7 minutes, until golden. Add tomato and sauté for 2 minutes. Add tomato paste and cook 2 to 3 minutes longer.

Stir in water, reduce heat to low and cook for 7 to 8 minutes. Stir in spices. Add olives and mushrooms and mix well. Cook on low heat 5 minutes longer, stirring occasionally.

Remove pan from heat. If you want the mixture to be thicker, add an additional tablespoon of tomato paste.

Yield: 4 servings.

Note: Good with white or brown rice

Recipe by Margalit Glazer

Irresistible Puréed Peas

2 tablespoons butter or
  margarine
1 onion, chopped
1 green pepper, finely chopped
6 cups frozen green peas
  (defrosting is not necessary)
$\frac{1}{2}$ cup water

$\frac{3}{4}$ teaspoon salt
pinch of black pepper
pinch of freshly grated nutmeg
2 tablespoons sour cream
  (optional)
chopped red pepper and fresh
  parsley, to garnish (optional)

Melt butter on medium heat in a skillet. Add onion and green pepper; cook for about 10 minutes, or until soft.

Add peas and water. Cover tightly and simmer on low heat, stirring often, until peas are almost tender, about 8 minutes. Uncover, increase heat to medium and continue to cook until water is evaporated and peas are very soft, stirring often. Stir in seasonings.

Puree in food processor until fairly smooth, scraping down sides of bowl as needed. Add sour cream, if using. Add more salt, pepper and nutmeg if needed.

Place in a serving dish and swirl the top. You may want to sprinkle with chopped red pepper and parsley.

Tip: You can make this ahead and place it in a microwave-safe serving dish. Cover and refrigerate. Reheat on Medium powder in the microwave, stirring every 2 or 3 minutes.

Yield: 6 to 8 servings.

Recipe by G.G.

Sweet Potato

Sweet potato offers many nutritional benefits for women because it is packed with nutrients that help prevent cervical tube defects, cervical and breast cancer, and osteoporosis. Besides, the sweet potato has no more fat than the potato.

- Leave skins on while cooking for the biggest fiber and nutrient gain.
- Bake them, boil them, grate them or mash them. Sweet potatoes take about 25 to 30 minutes to boil or about 1 hour to bake at 400°F (200°C), depending on size.

*Consider the sweet potato,
its nutrients may help prevent
cervical and breast cancer.*

Monda Rosenberg

Tiny Baby Potatoes

2 to 3 pounds red and white baby potatoes

2 to 3 tablespoons olive oil
Kosher salt or sea salt to taste

Preheat oven to 350°F.

Wash potatoes; dry well. Place in a greased baking dish or disposable aluminum foil pan. Drizzle olive oil over potatoes and sprinkle with salt. Mix well, making sure potatoes are well coated.

Roast at 450°F for one hour, shaking the pan several times during baking. Check for crispness and bake a little longer, if necessary. Roasting time will depend on the size of the potatoes.

Yield: 6 to 8 servings.

Recipe by Sharon London Liss

Potato Pudding

3 to 4 tablespoons oil	3 eggs, lightly beaten
1 medium onion	1 tablespoon flour
4 medium potatoes, peeled	salt and pepper to taste

Preheat oven to 425°F. Place oil in a 9-inch x 13-inch baking dish, using enough to cover the bottom. Place pan in oven and let oil heat while preparing the rest of the ingredients, about 5 minutes.

Grate onion and potatoes. Drain excess liquid. Add beaten eggs and flour; season with salt and pepper to taste.

Make sure oil is very hot, then pour mixture into pan and spread evenly. Oil will sizzle up around potato mixture.

Bake at 425°F for ½ hour. Reduce heat to 400°F and continue to bake another 30 to 45 minutes. Remove from oven and let cool. Cut into squares.

Reheat in 350°F oven for 15 minutes before serving.

Food Processor Method: Insert Steel Blade in processor. Cut onion in chunks and add through feed tube while machine is running. Remove cover; add eggs, flour, salt and pepper to work bowl. Pulse on and off, until well blended. Pour mixture into a large bowl. Insert Grater in processor, cut potatoes in chunks and grate. Add to egg mixture and proceed as above.

Yield: 10 to 12 servings.

Recipe by Lois Friedman Fine

My Mama's Latkas

2 medium onions, peeled
6 large Idaho potatoes
3 eggs

¼ to ¾ cup all-purpose flour
salt and pepper, to taste
canola oil, for frying

Process onions until finely minced. Remove from processor and place in a large bowl. Process the potatoes in two batches, until grated.

Combine potatoes with onions, eggs, salt and pepper and just enough flour to make a batter.

Heat oil in a large skillet on medium-high heat. For each pancake, drop 1 to 2 tablespoons batter into hot oil, depending on the size and thickness you like. (I prefer them smaller and I flatten them so they will be crispier.)

Fry latkas on each side until golden brown, about 2 to 3 minutes per side. Drain on paper towels. Place on a cookie sheet in a 200°F degree oven while frying remaining latkas. Then I arrange them in layers and freeze them.

Reheat uncovered in a 400°F oven for 10 minutes, until crispy. Serve with applesauce or sour cream.

Yield: about 3 dozen.

Tips: If you process the onions first, the potatoes will not discolour. To make these healthier, use a non-stick skillet and spray it with non-stick spray.

Recipe by G.G.

Zucchini Latkas

A low-carb alternative to regular latkas!

1 tablespoon olive or grapeseed oil
1 medium onion, minced
1 clove garlic, minced
2 pounds (500 grams) zucchini, shredded
1 red bell pepper, seeded and
  minced
3 eggs, lightly beaten

2 tablespoons flour
  (add a little more if mixture
  is too loose)
1 teaspoon salt
$1/4$ teaspoon pepper
$1/4$ cup canola oil, divided use
sour cream or Parmesan
  cheese, to garnish

Heat olive oil over medium heat in a large heavy skillet. Cook onion until tender, about 5 minutes. Add garlic, zucchini and bell pepper. Cook until zucchini softens, about 4 minutes, stirring occasionally. Remove from heat.

Drain in a strainer, squeezing out as much moisture as possible. Transfer to a bowl and stir in eggs, flour, salt and pepper.

Wipe skillet clean and heat 2 tablespoons canola oil over medium-high heat. When oil is hot, add a heaping tablespoon of batter to skillet for each pancake, flattening it with the back of the spoon. Fry latkas for 2 to 3 minutes on each side, until golden brown.

Drain on paper towels. Repeat with remaining batter and oil. Serve with sour cream or a sprinkling of Parmesan cheese.

Yield: about 12 pancakes (4 servings).

Recipe by G.G.

Couscous with Basil Veggies

1¼ cups chicken broth	2 large garlic cloves, minced
1 cup couscous	½ teaspoon pepper
¼ cup dried apricots, finely chopped	¼ teaspoon cumin
2 teaspoons olive oil	½ cup shredded fresh basil
3 cups sliced mixed vegetables (e.g., carrots, zucchini)	3 tablespoons fresh squeezed lime or lemon juice
	2 green onions, slice thinly

Microwave broth uncovered on HIGH power until it comes to a boil, about 2 to 3 minutes (or bring broth to a boil in a saucepan).

Stir in couscous and apricots. Cover and set aside until couscous is tender and broth has been absorbed, about 10 minutes.

Meanwhile, heat oil in a large non-stick skillet over medium heat. Add garlic and vegetables; sprinkle with pepper and cumin. Stir-fry for 3 to 4 minutes, until heated through. Remove from heat and stir in basil, juice and green onions.

Taste couscous and add more lemon juice and a pinch of salt if needed. Serve vegetables on top of couscous for a pretty presentation.

Yield: 4 servings.

Tip: This is a good dish with chicken, lamb or fowl. It only takes about 10 minutes to prepare and 5 minutes to cook.

Recipe by G.G.

Lemon Barley Pilaf With Raisins

2 tablespoons olive or canola oil
2 onions, finely chopped
3 celery stalks, finely chopped
1 cup pearl barley, rinsed and drained
2½ cups chicken or vegetable broth
1 teaspoons finely grated lemon zest
½ teaspoon dried oregano
salt and freshly ground pepper, to taste
¼ cup golden raisins (sultanas are best)
1 tablespoon lemon juice
2 tablespoons pine nuts
2 tablespoons chopped fresh parsley

In a wide heavy saucepan, heat olive oil over medium-high heat. Add onions and celery; sauté about 5 minutes, until softened and browned.

Add barley to pan, stirring to coat with oil. Add broth, lemon zest, oregano, salt and pepper. Bring to a boil. Reduce heat, cover and simmer, stirring occasionally, about 40 minutes or until barley is almost cooked through and most of liquid is absorbed.

Stir in raisins and lemon juice. Remove from heat and let stand for 5 minutes.

Toast pine nuts over medium heat for 5 to 7 minutes, or until golden brown. Gently stir pine nuts into pilaf along with parsley.

Yield: 8 servings.

Tip: Terrific with chicken and so healthy!

Recipe by G.G.

Never-Fail Basmati Rice

2 cups white basmati rice	dash of salt
2½ cups cold water	1 tbsp. oil

Rinse rice in cold water and drain completely. Place in a large saucepan; add 2½ cups cold water, salt and oil. Bring rice to a boil over high heat. Do not cover saucepan.

Immediately cover saucepan and move it to another burner that has been preheated on low. (Don't leave the pot on the original burner or the rice will cook too quickly, even if you lower the heat.)

Cook for 10 to 12 minutes. Test for doneness to be sure.

Yield: 6 to 8 servings.

Note: This method always produces fluffy, not sticky, rice

Recipe by Joni Seligman

Roasted Pepper Rice

This colourful side dish is excellent to serve at a barbecue and will feed a large crowd.

4 red peppers
2 green peppers
1 orange pepper
1 yellow pepper
2 large sweet onions
1 clove finely chopped garlic
½ cup olive oil

salt, pepper and oregano, to taste
2 cups basmati or long-grain rice (see Notes below)
2½ cups chicken broth (approximately)

Preheat oven to 400°F. Cut each pepper in half; discard the seeds and cores. Coarsely chop peppers and onions. (Try to cut them into pieces approximately the same size.)

In a large bowl, mix together garlic, olive oil, salt, pepper and oregano. Add vegetables and toss together until veggies are nicely coated. Transfer to a large baking sheet that has been sprayed with non-stick spray, spreading out veggies in a single layer.

Roast uncovered at 400°F for approximately 40 minutes. Check vegetables, stirring them occasionally. Veggies will soften and the tips may blacken a bit.

Cook rice in chicken broth, adding a pinch of salt if necessary. When rice is done, toss in veggies and enjoy along with your favourite barbequed main dish (burgers, steaks, chicken, etc.).

Yield: 10 to 12 servings.

Notes: For perfect rice, cook according to the method described in Never-Fail Basmati Rice (see page 175), substituting chicken broth for water. While veggies are roasting in the oven and rice is cooking, barbecue the main dish.

Recipe by Paula Carello

Oriental Rice and Wheat Berry Pilaf

$\frac{1}{2}$ cup wheat berries
$\frac{1}{2}$ cup wild rice
$\frac{1}{2}$ cup basmati rice
2 cloves garlic, finely minced
1 shallot, minced
2 tablespoons unsalted butter
 or margarine
$\frac{1}{2}$ cup currants
$\frac{1}{2}$ cup dried cranberries
3 tablespoons minced fresh
 cilantro
$\frac{1}{2}$ cup toasted pine nuts or
 sesame seeds

$\frac{1}{2}$ cup minced green onions

Sauce:
$3\frac{1}{2}$ cups chicken broth
3 tablespoons dry sherry
3 tablespoons light soy sauce
$1\frac{1}{2}$ tablespoons Oriental
 sesame oil
$\frac{1}{2}$ to $\frac{3}{4}$ teaspoon Chinese chili
 sauce
$\frac{1}{2}$ teaspoon salt
2 teaspoons grated orange
 zest

Soak wheat berries for 2 hours in cold water to cover completely. Drain well. Place wild rice in a sieve. Rinse under cold running water, stirring with your fingers until water runs clear. Drain well. Repeat with basmati rice, keeping the two rices separate.

Place a large saucepan over medium-high heat. Add garlic, shallot and butter. Sauté for 1 to 2 minutes, until butter sizzles. Add wheat berries and wild rice; stir to coat them well, about 5 minutes.

Sauce: Combine broth with sherry, soy sauce, sesame oil, chili sauce, salt and orange zest in a bowl.

Add sauce mixture and currants to saucepan and bring to a boil. Cover, reduce heat and simmer gently for 30 minutes. Stir in basmati rice and return to simmer. Continue cooking 20 to 30 minutes longer, or until water is absorbed and grains are soft.

Remove cover; stir in dried cranberries, green onions, cilantro and pine nuts or sesame seeds. Serve immediately.

Yield: 4 to 6 servings as a side dish.

Recipe by Vera Finkelstein

Cranberry Stuffing, Gloria's Adaptation

½ cup dried cranberries
¼ cup dry sherry
¼ teaspoon pepper
8 cups cut-up dry bread, with crusts (half cornbread and half whole wheat)
3 cloves garlic, minced
1 medium onion, chopped
2 stalks celery, chopped
1 cup chopped mushrooms (optional)

½ cup margarine or Earth Balance buttery spread, divided use
3 tablespoons chopped fresh parsley
1 teaspoon dried thyme
1 teaspoon dried sage
½ cup water
2 to 3 cups vegetable or chicken broth, as needed

Preheat oven to 350°F. Spray a large ovenproof casserole with non-stick spray.

Combine cranberries and sherry in a small bowl; stir well. Let stand at room temperature for 1 hour.

Meanwhile, place cut-up bread on a cookie sheet; bake at 350°F until lightly toasted, about 7 to 10 minutes.

In a large skillet, sauté garlic, onion, celery and mushrooms in ¼ cup margarine until tender, about 7 to 8 minutes. Add remaining ¼ cup margarine, cranberry-sherry mixture, parsley, thyme and sage. Mix well.

Place toasted bread cubes in a large bowl and add sautéed vegetable mixture. Add water and as much chicken or vegetable broth as needed to reach a soft consistency, perhaps 2 to 3 cups.

Transfer to prepared casserole and bake at 350°F for 25 minutes, covered.

Yield: about 2 quarts (8 cups).

Recipe by G.G.

BREAD, MUFFINS AND CAKES

Olive Bread

1 kg (2.2 pounds) flour (about 7 cups)	100 grams sliced pitted black olives, well-drained (about ½ cup)
1 tablespoon active dry yeast	1 tablespoon dried oregano
3 cups lukewarm water (approximately)	1 teaspoon salt
100 grams sliced pitted green olives, well-drained (about ½ cup)	3 teaspoons olive oil, to brush on loaves

In a large mixing bowl, mix together flour, yeast and lukewarm water with a wooden spoon. (If dough seems dry, add up to an additional 1/2 cup water, depending on the brand of flour used.) Continue kneading by hand about 10 minutes, until dough is smooth and elastic. Cover bowl with a clean towel and let stand at room temperature for 30 minutes to allow dough to rise.

Knead the dough again. Add green olives, black olives, oregano and salt to the dough. Moisten your hands in lukewarm water and knead the dough once again, until smooth and elastic. Divide the dough into 3 equal portions. Shape each piece of dough according to the shape desired for each loaf. Place shaped loaves onto a baking sheet lined with parchment paper. Be sure that paper is not greased. Brush the top of each loaf with a teaspoon of olive oil and sprinkle a bit of flour on top. Cover with a towel and let stand until loaves have doubled.

Fifteen minutes before you are ready to bake the loaves, preheat oven to 350°F. Bake loaves about 50 minutes, until bottom crust of the bread is lightly golden. Remove loaves from baking sheet and let cool.

Yield: 3 loaves. These freeze well.

Notes: This recipe contains no oil or eggs in the dough. Dough can also be kneaded in a mixer. To make it easier to knead the dough, always moisten your hands in lukewarm water first.

Recipe by Margalit Glazer

Bran Muffins

1 cup All-Bran cereal
1 cup milk
¼ cup applesauce
¼ cup oil
1 egg
¾ cup brown sugar, lightly
   packed

1 cup all-purpose flour, sifted
½ teaspoon baking powder
1 teaspoon baking soda
¼ teaspoon salt
1 teaspoon cinnamon
½ cup raisins
grated zest of 1 orange

Preheat oven to 425°F.

Combine cereal and milk in a large bowl and let stand for 15 minutes.

In the large bowl of an electric mixer, combine applesauce, oil, egg and brown sugar. Beat for 10 minutes, until light.

Sift together flour, baking powder, baking soda, salt and cinnamon. Add dry ingredients alternately with oil mixture to bran mixture. Stir just until blended. Stir in raisins and orange zest.

Fill greased or sprayed muffin tins ¾ full. Bake 10 to 12 minutes, or until muffins test done.

Yield: 12 to 14 large muffins.

Recipe by Nancy Posluns

Gigi's Corn Muffins

1 cup all-purpose flour	$\frac{1}{2}$ teaspoon salt
1 cup yellow cornmeal	1 cup milk
2 tablespoons turbinado (raw) sugar	$\frac{1}{2}$ cup (1/4 pound) melted butter (or Earth Balance)
2$\frac{1}{2}$ teaspoons baking powder	2 eggs

Preheat oven to 400°F. Grease twelve 3-inch muffin cups (or use paper liners).

In a large bowl, combine flour, cornmeal, sugar, baking powder and salt; mix well. Stir in milk until mix moistened. Add melted butter and eggs; mix until blended. Pour batter into prepared muffin cups.

Bake at 400°F for 15 to 20 minutes, or until a wooden toothpick inserted in the center comes out clean.

Yield: 12 muffins.

Recipe by Gigi Martinez

Apple or Peach Passion Cake

1 cup oil
4 eggs
2 cups sugar
½ cup + 2 tablespoons orange
   juice
3 teaspoons vanilla
3 cups all-purpose flour

2 teaspoons baking powder
1 can (19 ounces/540 ml)
   apple or peach passion pie
   filling (such as E.D. Smith)
2 teaspoons cinnamon
   (omit if using peach passion
   pie filling)

Preheat oven to 350°F. Grease a 9-inch x 13-inch pan (or line with parchment paper).

Beat oil, eggs and sugar together until light. Add orange juice and vanilla; mix well. Combine flour and baking powder; add to batter. (It will be quite thick.)

In another bowl, mix apple pie filling with cinnamon. Spread half the batter in bottom of pan. Spread filling over batter, then top with remaining batter.

Bake at 350°F for 1 to 1¼ hours. Test cake for doneness with a toothpick after 1 hour as some ovens are hotter than others.

Yield: 12 servings.

Recipe by Geetie Brown

German Apple Cake

Batter:
4 eggs
1 cup (½ pound) butter
1 cup sugar
1½ cups all-purpose flour
grated rind of 1 lemon

Apple Mixture:
2½ pounds apples (7 to 8 apples), peeled and cored
½ cup sugar
½ cup ground almonds

Preheat oven to 350°F. Grease a 12-inch spring form pan.

Beat eggs and butter until light. Add sugar and beat until smooth. Gradually add flour and lemon rind.

Meanwhile, cut apples into thin slices. Mix with sugar and almonds.

Spread batter evenly in pan. Top with apple mixture. Bake at 350°F for 1½ hours. Serve warm for best results. Good plain or topped with ice cream.

Yield: 12 servings.

Recipe by Anita Bender

Norene's Apple Lover's Cake

My father loved apples so much that he ate everything but the stems!
I know he would have loved this cake. The recipe comes from my
cookbook, The Food Processor Bible.

14 to 16 apples, peeled, quartered and cored	1 teaspoon vanilla extract (or 1 tablespoon brandy)
$\frac{1}{3}$ to $\frac{1}{2}$ cup sugar (or to taste)	2 eggs (or 1 egg plus 2 egg whites)
2 teaspoons ground cinnamon	
$\frac{1}{2}$ cup additional sugar	1 cup flour (half whole wheat flour can be used)
$\frac{1}{2}$ cup canola oil	
$\frac{1}{2}$ cup unsweetened applesauce	1 teaspoon baking powder
	$\frac{1}{4}$ teaspoon salt

Preheat oven to 350°F.

Slicer: Slice apples, using medium pressure. Place in a sprayed 9-inch x 13-inch glass baking dish, filling it nearly to the top. (Apples will shrink during baking.) Sprinkle with $\frac{1}{3}$ to $\frac{1}{2}$ cup sugar and cinnamon and mix well; spread evenly in pan.

Steel Blade: Process remaining $\frac{1}{2}$ cup sugar, oil, applesauce, vanilla extract and eggs for 1 minute, until well blended. Add flour, baking powder and salt; process with 3 or 4 quick on/offs, until blended. Pour batter evenly over apples. Bake about 1 hour, or until golden.

Yield: 12 to 15 servings. Cake gets soggy if frozen, but it's unlikely there will be any leftovers!

Note: Delicious served warm with ice cream or frozen yogurt.

Recipe by Norene Gilletz

Blueberry Bundt Cake

Filling:
3 cups blueberries, fresh or frozen
½ cup sugar mixed with 1 tablespoon cinnamon
1 tablespoon lemon juice

Batter:
3 cups all-purpose flour
2 cups sugar
1 tablespoon baking powder
1 teaspoon salt
½ cup oil
½ cup applesauce
4 eggs
¼ cup orange juice
1 tablespoon vanilla

Preheat oven to 375°F. Spray a 10-inch Bundt pan with non-stick spray.

Sprinkle blueberries with cinnamon-sugar and lemon juice. Mix lightly with spoon or rubber spatula.

In large mixing bowl, sift together flour, sugar, baking powder and salt. Using a spoon, make a well in the center by pushing the dry ingredients up the sides of the bowl.

Combine oil, applesauce, eggs, orange juice and vanilla and pour into the well. Mix until well blended. Pour ⅓ of batter into prepared pan. Top with half of blueberry filling. Repeat, ending with remaining ⅓ of batter.

Bake at 375°F for 60 to 75 minutes, until cake tests done. Let cool about 20 minutes before turning cake out of pan onto a cooling rack.

Yield: 12 to 15 servings.

Recipe by Nancy Posluns

Coconut Banana Cakes

½ cup sour cream
¼ teaspoon baking soda
2 ½ cups sifted cake flour
2 ¼ teaspoons baking powder
½ teaspoon salt
½ cup (¼ pound) butter
½ cup brown sugar, lightly packed
½ cup granulated sugar
2 eggs

1 ½ cups mashed ripe bananas (2 to 3 medium)
2 teaspoons pure vanilla
2 cups toasted coconut, divided use
1 cup (6 ounces/170 grams) chopped bittersweet chocolate or chocolate chips
icing sugar or melted bittersweet chocolate, to garnish

Preheat oven to 350°F. Grease one 8 inch x 4-inch loaf pan and one 4-inch x 2-inch mini loaf pan with non-stick spray.

Mix sour cream together with baking soda in a small bowl. Stir flour, baking powder and salt together in another small bowl.

In an electric mixer on medium speed, beat butter until soft. Gradually add both sugars. Beat until light and fluffy, about 5 to 8 minutes, scraping sides of bowl often with a rubber spatula. Add eggs one at a time, then add bananas, scraping sides of bowl between each addition. The mixture may look curdled - this is okay.

Add flour mixture all at once. To prevent flour from flying all over the place, turn the mixer on and off in quick spurts, just enough to move the beater gradually around the bowl. This also helps prevent overbeating, which would make the cake tough. Once the flour is almost all incorporated, fold in 1½ cups of toasted coconut, using a rubber spatula. Remove bowl from mixer and scrape batter off the beater. Sprinkle chopped chocolate over batter; fold it in gently.

Divide batter between both pans, filling them no more than ⅔ full. Sprinkle the tops with remaining coconut. Bake smaller cake for 20 to 25 minutes, until nicely peaked in the centre and golden brown. Bake larger cake an additional 20 to 25 minutes. A toothpick placed in the center will come out with a few crumbs clinging to it, or, when put to your ear, you hear tiny, slow popping sounds.

Let rest 10 minutes before removing from the pans onto a cooling rack. Dust with icing sugar before serving, or drizzle with melted chocolate.

Yield: 1 large and 1 small loaf (12 slices).

Recipe by Lisa Slater

Jimmy's Cinnamon-Topped Blueberry Bread

½ cup (¼ pound) unsalted
  butter, melted and cooled
  to lukewarm
1 cup sugar
2 eggs
2 cups all-purpose flour
1 teaspoon baking powder

pinch of salt
½ cup milk
2 cups fresh blueberries,
  rinsed and patted dry
cinnamon and sugar,
  for sprinkling

Preheat oven to 350°F. Grease and flour a 9-inch x 5-inch loaf pan.

Cream butter and sugar in an electric mixer until fluffy. Add eggs one at a time, beating well after each addition. Combine flour, baking powder and salt. Add half of flour mixture to batter and mix just until combined. Add milk to batter, then blend in remaining flour mixture. Remove beaters and fold in blueberries with a rubber spatula.

Spoon batter into prepared pan. Sprinkle top of batter with cinnamon and sugar. Bake at 350°F for 1¼ hours. When done, a cake tester should come out dry.

Remove pan from oven and let cool for 10 to 15 minutes. Loosen edges with a spatula, then invert pan and carefully remove bread. Cover with a clean towel and let sit for ½ day before slicing.

Yield: 1 loaf (10 to 12 slices).

Note: This is also delicious toasted.

Recipe by Anita Bender

Chocolate Chip Banana Cake

Batter:
1 cup (½ pound) butter, melted
2 cups granulated sugar
2 eggs
3 ripe bananas, mashed
2 teaspoons baking soda
1 cup sour cream

2 cups all-purpose flour
2 teaspoons baking powder

Topping:
1 cup (6 ounces/170 grams) chocolate chips
½ cup brown sugar, lightly packed

Preheat oven to 350°F. Spray a 9-inch x 13-inch baking pan with non-stick spray.

Batter: In a large bowl, combine butter, sugar and eggs. Beat for 4 to 5 minutes, until light. Add bananas and mix until well blended, about 1 minute. Dissolve baking soda in sour cream; add to batter along with flour and baking powder. Mix just until combined.

Topping: Mix chocolate chips and brown sugar together in a bowl.

Pour half the batter into prepared pan and spread evenly. Sprinkle with half the topping. Repeat with remaining batter and topping.

Bake at 350°F for 50 to 60 minutes, until topping starts to brown and cake tests done. Remove from oven and serve when cool.

Yield: 12 to 15 servings.

Recipe by G.G.

Chocolate Fudge Chip Cake

1 package (19 ounces/
  540 grams) Duncan Hines
  chocolate fudge cake mix
1 package (4-serving size)
  instant chocolate pudding
  mix
1 cup sour cream

1 cup water
¾ cup safflower or canola oil
3 eggs
1 cup (6 ounces/170 grams)
  semi-sweet chocolate chips
powdered sugar, for sprinkling

Preheat oven to 350°F. Grease and flour a 10-inch Bundt pan.

In a large bowl, combine cake mix, pudding mix, sour cream, water, oil and eggs. Beat with an electric mixer on low speed until batter is blended. Then beat on medium-high speed for 2 minutes. The batter will be fairly thick. Stir chocolate chips into batter by hand. Pour cake batter into prepared pan.

Bake at 350°F for about 1 hour, or until a toothpick inserted near the center comes out clean.

Cool cake on wire rack for 15 minutes. Invert cake onto a serving platter and cool completely. Sift powdered sugar over cake.

Yield: 16 servings.

Tip: I can't believe that this cake is not too sweet, just yummy!

Recipe by G.G.

Flourless Chocolate Cake

Excellent for those of you who are concerned about wheat allergies.

8 ounces (250 grams) bittersweet chocolate, chopped in small pieces $1/3$ cup light rum	1 teaspoon vanilla extract 8 eggs, separated 1 cup sugar (superfine is best), divided use

Preheat oven to 350°F. Butter a 10-inch spring form pan and line it with waxed paper. In a glass bowl, combine chopped chocolate, rum and vanilla extract. Microwave on Medium power for 2 to 3 minutes, stirring every minute, until melted. Let cool.

In an electric mixer, beat egg yolks with $1/2$ cup sugar until light and pale yellow in colour. In another bowl, beat egg whites with remaining $1/2$ cup sugar until stiff peaks form. Set aside. Fold cooled chocolate mixture into egg yolk mixture. Gently fold egg whites into chocolate/egg yolk mixture until well combined.

Pour batter into prepared spring form pan. Bake at 350°F for 40 minutes, or until a cake tester or toothpick comes out clean. Cool cake on cake rack.

Yield: 12 servings (224 calories per serving). Freezes well.

Raspberry Purée: 2 cups fresh raspberries (or a 10 ounce/284ml package frozen raspberries, thawed)	$1/3$ cup red currant jelly 2 tablespoons orange juice

Blend raspberries, jelly and orange juice in a food processor until smooth. Strain the sauce into a bowl to get rid of the raspberry seeds.

Serving Tip: Dust a large plate with icing sugar. Pour a spoonful of sauce in the center of the plate. Place a wedge of cake on the sauce. Garnish with extra berries, mint leaves and a puff of whipped cream.

Recipe by G.G.

Nana's Chocolate Roll

7 large eggs, separated (bring to room temperature after separating)	$\frac{1}{2}$ cup sugar, divided use
	1 $\frac{1}{3}$ cups heavy whipping cream (35%)
$\frac{1}{2}$ cup unsweetened cocoa powder	shaved chocolate curls, to garnish

Preheat oven to 375°F. Spray a jelly roll pan (12-inch x 18-inch x 1-inch) with non-stick spray. Line pan with waxed paper and spray with non-stick spray.

Blend egg yolks with cocoa and $\frac{1}{4}$ cup sugar in a large mixing bowl; beat until foamy. Beat egg whites with remaining $\frac{1}{4}$ cup sugar in a medium bowl until they form firm peaks. Gently fold whites into yolks. Spread mixture evenly in prepared pan.

Bake at 375°F about 20 minutes, then check for doneness. If sides of cake are firm and pulling away from edge of pan, it is done. If not, bake another couple of minutes.

Whip cream in a chilled bowl until stiff. (If desired, add 2 to 3 tablespoons of sugar.)

Cool cake for a few minutes, then turn out onto a clean towel that has been sprinkled with sugar. Carefully peel off waxed paper. Spread a very thin layer of whipped cream over cooled cake, using no more than one-quarter of the whipped cream. Roll into a log or jelly roll by grasping the edge of the towel and rolling. (Trust me, it works.) Then cover the outside of the cake with remaining whipped cream. Sprinkle with chocolate shavings and place on a serving platter.

Yield: Serves 6 to 8 normal people!

Note: Gary, Mike and Ronnie eat one whole roll, so I always have to make two! Incidentally, Nana invented this flourless cake, which is actually a fallen chocolate soufflé. Although it's not so good for diabetics, it's great for Pesach.

Recipe by Toba Weiss

Three-Layer Chocolate Cake

4 squares (4 ounces/
  115 grams) unsweetened
  chocolate
1/2 cup (1/4 pound) butter
2 cups sifted cake flour
2 cups sugar
1 1/2 teaspoons baking soda
pinch of salt

2 eggs, lightly beaten
1/2 cup sour cream
2 teaspoons vanilla
Chocolate Icing
  (recipe follows)
chocolate sprinkles,
  for garnishing

Preheat oven to 325°F. Grease three 9-inch round layer cake pans and coat lightly with flour, shaking out excess. (See Tip below.)

In the top of a double boiler, slowly melt chocolate together with butter over boiling water, stirring occasionally. Let cool.

Sift together flour, sugar, baking soda and salt into the large bowl of an electric mixer. Add cooled chocolate mixture and beat about 2 minutes, until well blended. Add eggs, sour cream and vanilla. Fold into chocolate mixture, then beat for 1 minute. Pour batter into cake pans, dividing evenly.

Bake at 325°F for 30 to 35 minutes, until cake layers test done. Remove from oven and let cool. Carefully remove layers one at a time from pans and place on separate plates.

Ice one cake layer with icing. Top with a second cake layer and spread it with icing. Add third cake layer. Spread top and sides of assembled cake with icing. Garnish with chocolate sprinkles.

Yield: 10 to 12 servings.

Tips: Try to find round tin pans that have a built-in cake remover. If you make the Chocolate Icing while the layers are baking, you won't have to wash the pot that you used to melt the chocolate and butter!

Recipe by Gladys Fogler

Chocolate Icing

2 squares (2 ounces/
  60 grams) unsweetened
  chocolate
3 tablespoons butter
¼ cup milk

1 egg
1 teaspoon vanilla
1 cup icing sugar
chocolate sprinkles, if desired

Put bowl and beaters in refrigerator to chill thoroughly before you begin.

Melt chocolate and butter in the top of a double boiler, stirring occasionally. Remove from heat. Add milk and stir well, until thick. Let cool, then pour into chilled bowl from the refrigerator. Add egg, vanilla and icing sugar; beat until stiff. If you have trouble, put bowl, along with icing and beaters, back in refrigerator to chill.

Yield: To fill and frost three 9-inch layers.

Recipe by Gladys Fogler

*Forget love... I'd rather fall
in chocolate!*
Author Unknown

Crumb Cake

2 cups all-purpose flour
1 cup sugar
½ cup (¼ pound) butter
1 teaspoon baking soda
1 cup sour cream (or sour milk)

1 egg
1 teaspoon pastry spices (e.g., cloves, allspice)
1 teaspoon cinnamon
¾ cup raisins

Preheat oven to 350°F. Spray an 8-inch x 8-inch square baking pan with non-stick spray.

Combine flour, sugar and butter in a large mixing bowl; mix together until fine crumbs are formed. Remove ¾ cup of the crumb mixture and set aside.

Dissolve baking soda in sour cream or sour milk. Let stand 2 to 3 minutes.

Using either an electric mixer or hand beater, mix remaining crumb mixture with remaining ingredients except the raisins. Mix well. Fold in raisins.

Pour batter into prepared pan and spread evenly. Top with reserved crumb mixture. Bake at 350°F for 35 to 40 minutes, until cake tests done.

Yield: 9 servings.

Recipe by Pauline Toker

Excellent Bourbon Cake

Cake:
8 candied cherries
½ cup chopped walnuts
1 package (19 ounces/540 grams) Duncan Hines yellow cake mix

1 package (4-serving size) instant coconut or pistachio pudding mix
1 cup milk (or lactaid)
4 eggs
1½ cups canola oil

Preheat oven to 350°F. Grease and flour a 10-inch Bundt pan. Place the cherries and nuts in bottom of pan.

In a large bowl, combine cake mix, pudding mix, milk, eggs and oil. Beat for 2 minutes, until well blended. Pour mixture into pan.

Bake at 350°F for 45 minutes, or until cake tests done. A toothpick inserted near the center should come out clean. Meanwhile, prepare Bourbon Mixture.

Bourbon Mixture:
½ cup (¼ pound) butter

½ cup bourbon
½ cup sugar (scant)

In a saucepan, combine butter, bourbon and sugar. Bring to a boil.

Remove cake from oven and pour half of bourbon mixture over the warm cake while it is still in the pan. Cool cake on a rack for 1 hour. Invert cake onto a serving platter and pour the remaining bourbon mixture over cake.

Yield: 16 servings.

Tip: Another Bundt cake hit! Great for New Year's Eve or holidays. Rich but divine!

Recipe by G.G.

Mother Molly's Secret Honey Cake

1 cup tea (or ¼ cup cognac plus tea to equal 1 cup)
1 teaspoon baking soda
4 eggs
1 cup granulated sugar
1 cup brown sugar, lightly packed
1 cup honey
1 cup vegetable oil
1 teaspoon vanilla
grated rind of a lemon
3 cups all-purpose flour
2 teaspoons baking powder
½ teaspoon allspice
½ teaspoon cinnamon
½ teaspoon nutmeg
¼ teaspoon salt
1 cup raisins
¾ cup roasted almonds, to garnish

Preheat oven to 300°F. Grease a 9-inch x 13-inch baking pan or two 9-inch x 5-inch loaf pans. Line pan(s) with waxed paper, then grease pan(s) once again.

Dissolve baking soda in tea and let stand while you prepare the batter.

In a large mixing bowl, combine eggs with both sugars; beat well. Add honey, oil, vanilla and lemon rind; mix well. Combine flour, baking powder, spices and salt. Add flour mixture to batter alternately with tea and mix just until blended.

Stir raisins into batter, or sprinkle them on top after you put batter into pan(s). Sprinkle roasted almonds on top.

Bake at 300°F for 1½ hours, or until cake tests done. Enjoy!

Yield: 16 to 18 servings.

Recipe by Sandi Samuels

The Guttman Lemon Juice Cake

This recipe comes from Esther Lipman.

1 package (19 ounces/ 540 grams) yellow cake mix	½ cup orange juice
1 package (4-serving size) lemon jello	½ cup water
4 eggs	juice of ½ a lemon
	½ cup corn oil

Preheat oven to 350°F.

Combine all ingredients in a bowl and beat for 2 minutes, until well mixed. Pour batter into an ungreased 9-inch x 13-inch rectangular baking pan (or two 8-inch round pans).

Bake at 350°F. If you are baking this in a rectangular pan, baking time will be 40 to 45 minutes. If you are baking this in two pans, baking time will be 25 to 30 minutes.

While cake is baking make the glaze.

Glaze:	2 tablespoons melted butter
1 cup powdered sugar	1 tablespoon water
½ cup lemon juice	

Combine all ingredients for glaze and mix until smooth. When cake is done, immediately poke holes all over the cake and pour the glaze over it.

Tip: Easy and so good!

Yield: 16 servings.

Recipe by G.G.

Pecan Nut Roll

6 egg yolks
¾ cup sugar
1 teaspoon baking powder
1½ cups grated pecans
6 egg whites

1½ cups heavy whipping
cream (35%)
3 to 4 tablespoons additional
sugar (to taste)

Preheat oven to 350°F. Grease a jelly roll pan (12-inch x 18-inch x 1-inch). Line pan with parchment paper, then grease the parchment paper.

Beat egg yolks together with sugar until thick. Mix baking powder together with pecans and fold into yolk mixture.

Whip egg whites until stiff but not dry. Fold into batter. Spread batter evenly in prepared pan. Bake at 350°F for 20 minutes, until cake tests done.

Cover with a damp towel and place in refrigerator for several hours to chill. Turn cake out onto towel and carefully peel off paper.

In a chilled bowl, whip cream until stiff. Add sugar to taste. Spread whipped cream on cake and roll up like a jelly roll. Place on a serving plate and refrigerate until serving time.

Yield: 8 servings.

Recipe by Phyllis Crystal

Chocolate Zucchini Cake

¼ cup butter
½ cup vegetable oil
1¾ cups sugar
2 eggs
1 teaspoon vanilla
½ cup buttermilk or sour milk
2½ cups all-purpose flour

¼ cup unsweetened cocoa powder
½ teaspoon baking powder
½ teaspoon cinnamon
½ teaspoon cloves
2 cups grated zucchini
¼ cup chocolate chips

Preheat oven to 325°F. Grease and flour a 10-inch Bundt pan or a 9-inch x 13-inch baking pan.

Combine butter, oil, sugar, eggs, vanilla and buttermilk in a large mixing bowl. Cream thoroughly, until well mixed. Sift flour, cocoa, baking powder, cinnamon and cloves together; add them gradually to the creamed mixture. Mix in zucchini and chocolate chips.

Pour batter into prepared baking pan, spreading evenly. Bake at 325°F for 45 minutes, until cake tests done. If using a Bundt pan, let cool for 15 to 20 minutes before inverting pan and removing cake.

Yield: 12 to 15 servings. Delicious!

Note: A favourite recipe adapted from The Best of Bridge.

Recipe by Dr. Ricky Pasternak

Zucchini Zip Loaves

No one believes that there is zucchini in these delicious loaves.

3 eggs
1 cup canola oil
2 cups sugar
1 teaspoon vanilla
2 cups finely shredded
  zucchini (well-packed)

2½ cups all-purpose flour
1 teaspoon salt
2 teaspoons nutmeg
1 teaspoon baking soda
½ teaspoon baking powder
½ cup chopped nuts (optional)

Preheat oven to 325°F. Line two 9-inch x 5-inch loaf pans with parchment paper.

In an electric mixer, beat eggs, oil, sugar, vanilla and zucchini on low speed. Add remaining ingredients and blend well. Batter will be quite thin. Fill pans 2/3 full.

Bake at 325°F for one hour. Test with a cake tester to make sure they are fully baked. When done, let cool for 10 minutes, then invert onto a cooling rack, peel off parchment paper and let cool completely.

Yield: 2 loaves (20 to 24 slices). Freezes well.

Recipe by Geetie Brown

COOKIES AND SQUARES

Brooky's Cookies

1 cup (½ pound) butter	1½ cups all-purpose flour
1 cup sugar	3 teaspoons baking powder
1 egg	½ teaspoon salt
1 teaspoon vanilla	5 cups Special K cereal

Preheat oven to 350°F. Grease or spray a large cookie sheet.

Cream butter until light; gradually add sugar and blend well. Add egg and vanilla; mix well. Sift together flour, baking powder and salt; add to batter. Place cereal in a resealable plastic bag and crush coarsely. Add to batter and mix well.

Drop from a teaspoon onto prepared cookie sheet. Press each cookie as flat as possible with a fork dipped in cold water.

Bake each batch at 350°F about 10 minutes, until golden.

Yield: 6 to 8 dozen. Freezes well.

Recipe by Brooky Robins

Chocolate Cookies

4 squares (4 ounces/
115 grams) unsweetened
chocolate, chopped
6 tablespoons unsalted butter,
cut up
2 cups (12 ounces/340 grams)
semi-sweet chocolate chips,
divided use

$\frac{1}{2}$ cup all-purpose flour
2 tablespoons unsweetened
cocoa powder
$\frac{1}{4}$ teaspoon baking powder
$\frac{1}{2}$ teaspoon salt
1 cup sugar
3 large eggs
1 $\frac{1}{2}$ teaspoons vanilla

Preheat oven to 350°F. Line cookie sheets with parchment paper.

Combine chocolate, butter and 1 cup chocolate chips in a saucepan. Melt over low heat, stirring frequently. Remove from heat and let cool.

Stir together flour, cocoa, baking powder and salt.

In an electric mixer, beat together sugar, eggs and vanilla until pale and frothy, about 2 minutes. Mix in melted chocolate mixture, then add flour mixture at low speed. Stir in remaining cup of chocolate chips. Cover bowl and refrigerate dough about 2 hours.

Shape chilled dough into 1-inch balls. (Use a teaspoon to scoop out the dough and wet your hands for easier handling.) Arrange on prepared cookie sheets.

Bake in batches on middle rack of oven at 350°F about 10 minutes, until puffed and set. Cookies will be soft in the center. Transfer to racks to cool.

Yield: about 5 dozen.

Recipe by Mayta Markson

Great Chocolate Chip Cookies

1 cup (½ pound) butter, softened
1 cup brown sugar, lightly
  packed
¾ cup granulated sugar
2 eggs

1 teaspoon vanilla
2 cups all-purpose flour
1 teaspoon baking soda
½ teaspoon salt
2 cups semi-sweet chocolate
  chips

Preheat oven to 350°F. Grease cookie sheets. (I always work with 2 to speed things up.)

Cream butter with brown sugar and granulated sugar until light and fluffy. Add eggs and vanilla and mix well.

Sift dry ingredients together. Stir into batter, mixing thoroughly. Add chocolate chips to batter and mix well.

Drop batter from a teaspoon onto a greased cookie sheet. (Now, here's the trick!) Wet your fingers and flatten each cookie thinly.

Bake at 350°F for 5 for 7 minutes, until golden brown. Watch carefully to prevent burning. Leave cookies on cookie sheet for 3 to 4 minutes to set before removing them with a spatula.

Yield: about 5 dozen.

Tip: It took me many years to match my friend Carol Permutter's chocolate chip cookies, but I have, and they are almost as thin and crisp as hers!

Recipe by G.G.

Florentines

½ cup (¼ pound) unsalted butter
½ cup brown sugar, lightly packed
2½ tablespoons light corn syrup
½ cup all-purpose flour

1½ cups mixed candied fruit
½ cup sliced almonds
½ cup chopped pecans
1 cup (6 ounces/170 grams) semi-sweet chocolate, melted (for drizzling)

Preheat oven to 325°F. Line a large cookie sheet with parchment paper.

In the top of a double boiler, melt butter. Stir in brown sugar and corn syrup and cook until bubbly. Remove from heat and stir in flour, candied fruit, almonds and pecans.

Drop mixture from a teaspoon onto prepared cookie sheet about 3 to 4 inches apart. Be sure to leave lots of room between each cookie as they spread during baking. Wet your hand and flatten each cookie.

Bake each batch at 325°F about 15 to 20 minutes, until edges are light brown. Let cool on pan about 10 minutes, then remove from cookie sheet and transfer to a rack. Drizzle with melted chocolate.

Yield: 3 dozen.

Recipe by Shaynka Farber

Ruth's Mandelbroit

2 eggs	1 cup crushed toasted almonds
³/₄ cup oil	½ cup chocolate chips
1 cup sugar	cinnamon-sugar mixture
2 cups all-purpose flour	(1 tablespoon cinnamon
2 teaspoons baking powder	mixed with ¼ cup sugar)
1 cup crushed corn flakes	

Preheat oven to 350°F. Line 2 cookie sheets with parchment paper.

In a large bowl, mix eggs and oil until light. Add sugar and mix well. Add flour, baking powder, corn flakes, almonds and chocolate chips. Mix well.

Form 2 long, narrow logs on each cookie sheet. Sprinkle with cinnamon/sugar mixture. Bake at 350°F for 30 minutes, until golden.

Remove pans from oven. Slice logs while hot and spread out slices on cookie sheets. Shut off oven; place mandelbroit back in oven for 15 to 20 minutes to dry.

Yield: about 4 dozen.

Recipe by Ruth Garbe

Miriam's Mandelbroit

1 cup toasted almonds, crushed	dash of salt
3 eggs	1 cup corn flakes
1 cup canola or vegetable oil	$\frac{1}{2}$ cup chocolate chips, raisins or cranberries (optional)
1 cup sugar	cinnamon-sugar mixture
2$\frac{1}{2}$ to 3 cups whole wheat flour	(1 tablespoon cinnamon mixed with $\frac{1}{4}$ cup sugar)
3 teaspoons baking powder	

Preheat oven to 350°F. Line cookie sheet with parchment paper.

If using whole almonds, place in food processor and process until coarsely crushed, using quick on/offs.

Beat eggs in an electric mixer until light. Add oil and sugar; mix well. Slowly add 2 $\frac{1}{2}$ cups flour, baking powder and salt. Mix in corn flakes and almonds. If desired, add chocolate chips, raisins or cranberries. If dough is too sticky, add additional flour as needed.

Oil your hands for easier handling. Form mixture into three long, narrow rolls on prepared cookie sheet. Bake at 350°F for 20 minutes, until golden brown.

Remove from oven and let cool for 15 minutes. Then slice on the diagonal. Turn cut pieces on their side and sprinkle with cinnamon-sugar mixture. Place in 225°F oven for 1 hour.

Yield: about 5 dozen.

Recipe by Miriam Rubin

Pearl's Melba Toasted Almond Slices

This is a favourite low-fat cookie from Pearl Mekler.

4 egg whites
½ cup sugar
½ teaspoon vanilla
1 tablespoon lemon or orange
  juice
grated rind of ½ lemon

2 tablespoons oil
¾ cup + 1 tablespoon flour
¼ teaspoon salt
½ cup toasted almonds
½ cup dried cranberries
  and/or raisins

Preheat oven to 350°F. Line a loaf pan with parchment paper (or use an aluminum ice cube tray, but remove the dividers first)!

Beat egg whites until frothy. Gradually add sugar and beat until stiff. Combine vanilla, juice, rind and oil; fold into egg white mixture. Stir in flour and salt. Fold almonds, cranberries and/or raisins into mixture. Pour into prepared pan.

Bake at 350°F for 30 to 35 minutes, until golden. Cool slightly, then invert and remove loaf from pan. Peel off parchment paper. Wrap loaf in a tea towel and let cool. Refrigerate or freeze overnight.

Using a very sharp knife, cut into thin slices. Arrange slices in a single layer on a foil-lined baking sheet. Bake at 300°F about 30 minutes, until golden.

Yield: about 3 dozen.

Recipe by Nancy Posluns

Moon Cookies

4 eggs
1 cup oil
1 cup white sugar
Juice of ½ orange (or less than
  ⅓ cup orange juice)
4 cups all-purpose flour

2 teaspoons baking powder
½ teaspoon baking soda
pinch of salt
1 cup poppy seeds
sugar for sprinkling, if desired

Preheat oven to 350°F. Line cookie sheets with parchment paper.

Combine eggs, oil and sugar in a large mixing bowl; beat well. Add orange juice; mix well. Combine dry ingredients and add to egg mixture along with poppy seeds; mix well.

Divide dough into six pieces. Roll out each portion very thinly on a floured board. Cut into desired shapes with cookie cutters or a glass. Sprinkle dough lightly with sugar, then pierce with a fork. (This prevents dough from bubbling while baking.)

Transfer cookies to prepared cookie sheets. Bake in batches at 350°F for 12 to 15 minutes, or until golden brown. Baking time will depend on how thin you roll the dough.

Yield: about 7 to 8 dozen. Recipe can be cut in half, if desired.

Recipe by Geetie Brown

Oatmeal Raisin Cookies

½ cup (¼ pound) butter,
  softened
½ cup granulated sugar
½ cup packed brown sugar
1 egg
1 cup whole wheat flour

1 cup rolled oats
  (quick-cooking)
¼ cup wheat germ
1 teaspoon baking powder
1 teaspoon baking soda
1 cup raisins

Preheat oven to 350°F. Lightly grease cookie sheets.

In a large mixing bowl, cream butter with both sugars. Beat in egg. Combine flour, oats, wheat germ, baking powder and baking soda. Stir dry ingredients into creamed mixture and blend well. Stir in raisins.

Drop mixture from a tablespoon onto prepared cookie sheets. Flatten each cookie slightly with a floured fork.

Bake at 350°F about 12 minutes, or until light golden.

Yield: 3 dozen.

Recipe by Ruth Garbe

Toffee Cookies

1 cup (½ pound) butter
1 cup brown sugar, lightly
   packed
1 egg yolk
1 cup all-purpose flour

1 cup (6 ounces/170 grams)
   chocolate chips
⅔ cup chopped pecans or
   walnuts

Preheat oven to 350°F.

Beat butter with brown sugar until light. Add egg yolk and mix well. Blend in flour.

Spread batter evenly onto an ungreased cookie sheet with sides (10-inch x 15-inch x 1-inch). Bake at 350°F for 20 minutes, until golden.

Remove from oven and sprinkle with chocolate chips. When chips are melted, spread chocolate evenly over top with a spatula. Sprinkle with nuts. Cut into diamond shapes while still warm.

Yield: 2½ to 3 dozen.

Recipe by Lois Friedman Fine

Toffee Fingers

27 graham crackers
1¼ cups butter
1 cup brown sugar, lightly
packed
1 cup (6 ounces/170 grams)
chocolate chips, melted

1 package (4 ounces/
125 grams/1 cup) slivered
almonds (or 2 teaspoons
sesame seeds)

Preheat oven to 350°F. Cover a large rimmed baking sheet completely with aluminum foil.

Arrange graham crackers in a single layer on baking sheet.

In a saucepan, melt butter on medium heat. Add brown sugar, stirring until melted. Stir in almonds or sesame seeds and spread immediately over graham wafers.

Bake at 350°F about 9 minutes, or until very bubbly. Remove from oven and drizzle melted chocolate over top. Cool completely. Cut into finger shapes with a sharp knife. Store in the freezer.

Yield: about 3 dozen.

Note: Substitute any nuts you like for the almonds.

Recipe by Margaret Wayne

Best Ever Brownies

½ cup (¼ pound) butter	1 teaspoon vanilla
2 ounces (2 squares/	2 eggs
60 grams) unsweetened	½ cup all-purpose flour,
chocolate	sifted
1 cup sugar	pinch of salt

Preheat oven to 350°F. Grease an 8-inch x 8-inch square baking pan.

Melt butter and chocolate over low heat, stirring frequently. Remove from heat. Add sugar and vanilla; mix well. Add eggs one at a time, stirring well after each addition. Stir in flour and salt.

Pour batter into prepared baking pan and spread evenly. Bake at 350°F for 20 to 25 minutes, until set. Let cool, then cut into squares.

Yield: 25 squares.

Recipe by Jan Krock

I want to have a good body,
but not as much as I want dessert.
Jason Love

Brownie Torte

This is so simple to make and is a really good chocolate fix.

1 cup (6 ounces/170 grams) chocolate chips, divided use
2½ tablespoons butter, cut in pieces
1 egg

½ cup sugar
1 teaspoon vanilla extract
2 tablespoons flour
½ cup chopped walnuts

Preheat oven to 350°F. Butter and flour a 7-inch or 8-inch pie dish.

Melt ¾ cup of chocolate chips with butter in a large pan set over hot water; stir frequently.

In a bowl, whisk together egg, sugar and vanilla until foamy. Whisk egg mixture into chocolate mixture. Fold in flour. Stir in nuts and remaining ¼ cup chocolate chips.

Bake at 350°F for 15 to 20 minutes, until a knife comes out clean. (It's better if it is underbaked to keep it moist.)

Yield: 6 to 8 servings.

Recipe by Anne Estern

Chocolate Squares (Unbaked)

½ cup brown sugar, lightly
  packed
½ cup corn syrup
1 cup peanut butter
1 teaspoon vanilla extract

1 cup corn flakes
2 cups rice krispies
1 cup (6 ounces/170 grams)
  chocolate chips

Lightly grease a 9-inch x 13-inch baking dish.

Combine brown sugar and corn syrup in a large pot. Heat on low, stirring constantly, until melted. Remove from heat.

Stir in peanut butter, vanilla, corn flakes, rice krispies and chocolate chips. Spread mixture evenly in prepared baking dish. Cut into squares with a sharp knife.

Yield: 48 squares.

Recipe by Shaynka Farber

Stressed spelled backwards is desserts.
Coincidence? I think not!

Author Unknown

Date Squares

2 cups pitted dates	1 cup brown sugar, lightly
2 cups orange juice	packed
2 cups rolled oats	1 teaspoon baking soda
1 cup all-purpose flour	¾ cup melted butter

Preheat oven to 350°F. Grease a 9-inch x 13-inch baking pan.

Combine dates and orange juice in a saucepan. Simmer slowly for 30 minutes or until dates are softened. Add more juice if necessary.

Combine rolled oats, flour, brown sugar, baking soda and butter in a bowl. Mix together until crumbly. Press half of crumb mixture into the bottom of prepared pan. Spread date mixture over base. Sprinkle rest of crumb mixture over date filling.

Bake at 350°F for 40 to 45 minutes, until golden.

Yield: 48 squares.

Recipe by Diane Oille

Geraldine's Lemon Squares

Base: **2 cups sifted all-purpose flour**
1 cup butter, cut in chunks   **½ cup confectioners' sugar**

Preheat oven to 350°F. Lightly grease a cookie sheet with sides (about 10-inches x 15-inches x 1-inch).

Combine butter, flour and sugar in a food processor until mixture is crumbly. (You could also mix it by hand, like making pastry.) Press firmly into prepared pan until evenly spread. Bake at 350°F for 20 minutes, until golden. Prepare filling while crust is baking.

Filling: **4 tablespoons lemon juice**
4 eggs   **(I use green limes)**
1 cup sugar   **4 tablespoons flour**
1 teaspoon baking soda   **confectioner's sugar**

Beat eggs until they are frothy and light yellow. Add the sugar little by little until the mixture forms a ribbon. Add lemon juice, flour and baking soda and mix a little longer on the lowest speed of your mixer, until blended.

Pour over baked crust. Bake 20 minutes longer, until golden and set. Dust with confectioner's sugar. When it is cool, cut into squares.

Yield: 48 squares.

Recipe by Geraldine Morales

Lemony Cranberry Squares

Crust:
2 cups all-purpose flour
½ cup sugar
½ cup (¼ pound) unsalted butter, at room temperature
¼ teaspoon salt

Filling:
3 eggs
2 cups sugar
⅓ cup freshly squeezed lemon juice
2 cups frozen or fresh whole cranberries (not canned)
2 cups shredded unsweetened coconut
2 tablespoons flour
1 teaspoon baking powder
¼ teaspoon salt

Preheat oven to 350°F. Butter a 9-inch x 13-inch glass baking pan.

Crust: Mix together flour, sugar, butter and salt until crumbly. Press mixture into prepared pan. Bake at 350°F for 20 minutes until golden. Remove pan from oven. Reduce temperature to 325°F. While crust is baking, prepare the filling.

Filling: Combine eggs, sugar, lemon juice, cranberries and coconut in a mixing bowl; mix well. Stir in flour, baking powder and salt. Pour mixture over crust and spread evenly.

Bake at 325°F for 40 to 45 minutes, until the center is firm. Refrigerate until firm. Cut into squares. Keep refrigerated.

Yield: 48 squares. Freezes well.

Recipe by Joni Seligman

Salted Peanut Chews

Base:
1½ cups all-purpose flour
⅔ cup brown sugar, firmly packed
½ teaspoon baking powder
½ teaspoon salt
¼ teaspoon baking soda
½ cup margarine or butter, softened
1 teaspoon vanilla
2 egg yolks
3 cups miniature marshmallows

Topping:
⅔ cup corn syrup
¼ cup margarine or butter
2 teaspoons vanilla extract
1 (10 ounces/300 grams) package peanut butter chips
2 cups rice krispies
2 cups salted peanuts

Preheat oven to 350°F.

Base: In the large bowl of an electric mixer, combine all ingredients except for marshmallows. Mix at low speed until crumbly. Press firmly into the bottom of an ungreased 9-inch x 13-inch baking pan. Bake at 350°F for 12 to 15 minutes, until light golden brown.

Remove from oven and immediately sprinkle with marshmallows. Return pan to oven. Bake 1 to 2 minutes longer, or until marshmallows just begin to puff. Cool while preparing topping.

Topping: In a large saucepan, combine all topping ingredients except for rice krispies and peanuts. Heat mixture just until chips are melted and mixture is smooth, stirring constantly. Remove from heat and stir in cereal and peanuts. Immediately spoon the warm topping over the marshmallows and spread evenly.

Refrigerate 45 minutes, or until firm. Cut into squares.

Yield: 48 squares.

Recipe by Shaynka Farber

Spiced Sugared Nuts

8 cups nuts (pecans, walnuts, almonds or cashews, or a mixture of nuts)
$^3/_4$ cup sugar
1 teaspoon cinnamon
$^1/_2$ teaspoon salt

$^1/_4$ teaspoon nutmeg
$^1/_4$ teaspoon allspice
$^1/_4$ teaspoon cloves
1 egg white
$2^1/_2$ tablespoons water

Preheat oven to 275°F. Lightly grease a foil-lined cookie sheet.

Combine all ingredients together in a large bowl; mix well. Spread out on prepared cookie sheet.

Bake at 275°F for 50 to 55 minutes, stirring occasionally. Store in a tightly covered container.

Yield: about 8 cups.

Recipe by Marilyn Himmel

DESSERTS

Chocolate Pots de Crème à la Minute

Chocolate Mixture:
1½ cups heavy whipping cream (35%)
1 teaspoon instant coffee granules
¼ cup sugar
1 cup (6 ounces/170 grams) bittersweet chocolate, chopped
2 eggs

2 egg yolks
1 tablespoon Kalhua (optional)

Topping:
½ cup heavy whipping cream (35%)
1 tablespoon sugar
1 tablespoon Kalhua
cinnamon, cocoa and/or chocolate curls (for garnish)

Preheat oven to 300°F. Spray 4 demitasse cups or 4-ounce custard cups with vegetable spray. Have 2 cups of boiling water ready to pour into a roasting pan.

Chocolate Mixture: Place whipping cream, instant coffee, sugar and chocolate in a small saucepan over low heat. Heat just enough to melt the chocolate, stirring often. Remove from heat. Whisk in the eggs, egg yolks and Kalhua. Pour into prepared demitasse cups. Place filled cups in a roasting pan and place pan in the oven. Pour boiling water halfway up the sides. Cover roasting pan completely with foil. Bake at 300°F about 15 minutes, or until a quarter-sized circle in the center becomes jiggly, but is not completely liquid.

Remove pan from oven and remove foil immediately. Let cups sit in hot water about 5 minutes longer. Remove cups and let sit at room temperature for no more than 15 minutes if you want to serve them warm. They can just as easily be made ahead. Cool to room temperature, then place in refrigerator to chill completely, at least 4 hours.

Topping: Whip cream with sugar and Kalhua until soft peaks form. Top chocolate with whipped cream. Garnish with a dusting of cinnamon, cocoa and/or some chocolate curls. Delicious served warm or cold.

Yield: 4 servings.

Recipe by Lisa Slater

Crême Brulée

This is the best recipe I have ever tried for Crême Brulée.

3 cups heavy whipping cream (35%)	**2 teaspoons vanilla**
	6 egg yolks
6 tablespoons fruit sugar or granulated sugar	**½ cup light brown sugar, lightly packed**

Preheat oven to 300°F. (If you have a hot oven, reduce the temperature to 250°F.)

Heat cream in the top of a double boiler. Stir in sugar and vanilla. Beat egg yolks until light. Slowly pour beaten yolks into hot cream mixture, stirring constantly.

Pour mixture into a greased baking dish. Place in a larger baking pan and add water to come 1-inch up the sides.

Bake at 300°F for 40 to 50 minutes, depending on your oven. To test for doneness, insert a knife near the edge of the dish. If the knife comes out clean, the custard will be firm all the way through when cooled. Chill if desired.

Sprinkle brown sugar over custard, right to the very edges of the dish. Put under a hot broiler just long enough for sugar to melt and form a crust, about 4 minutes. Watch carefully to prevent scorching. Serve warm or chilled.

Yield: 6 to 8 servings.

Recipe by Joanne Smith Cutler

Delicious Rice Pudding

4 cups milk (2%)
¼ cup granulated sugar
¼ cup brown sugar (scant)
½ cup long-grain white rice,
  rinsed and drained
2 eggs

1 teaspoon vanilla
½ cup raisins
½ cup dried apricots,
  if desired
cinnamon and nutmeg, to taste
pinch of cloves, if desired

In a large saucepan, combine milk, both sugars and rice; mix well. Cook over medium-low heat for 35 to 45 minutes, until rice is soft and pudding mixture has thickened, stirring often. Skim occasionally.

In a small bowl, beat eggs lightly. Add about 2 tablespoons of hot milk from pudding mixture and stir well. Remove saucepan from heat and quickly stir in eggs. Return saucepan to heat and cook 3 to 5 minutes longer, stirring constantly. Stir in vanilla, raisins and apricots, if using.

Spoon the pudding mixture into serving bowls. Sprinkle with cinnamon, nutmeg and cloves, if using. Delicious served hot or cold. The pudding will become even thicker when it cools.

Yield: 4 to 6 servings.

Recipe by Joanne Smith Cutler

Lemon Meringue Dream

6 extra-large eggs, separated	$\frac{1}{3}$ cup lemon juice
1 teaspoon white vinegar	$\frac{1}{3}$ cup sugar
$\frac{1}{8}$ teaspoon salt	grated rind of 1 lemon
$1\frac{1}{2}$ cups fruit sugar (superfine)	1 cup heavy whipping cream
$\frac{1}{4}$ cup toasted slivered almonds	(35%)

Preheat oven to 250°F. Grease and flour two 9-inch round pans.

Meringue Shells: In an electric mixer, beat egg whites until foamy. Add vinegar and salt. Beat at high speed until soft peaks form. Gradually add fruit sugar and continue to beat for 7 minutes, until stiff peaks are formed.

Divide meringue mixture evenly between prepared pans. Use the back of a spoon to shape the meringue into soft peaks. Sprinkle one meringue shell with slivered almonds. (This will be the top layer.)

Bake at 250°F for 1 hour and 20 minutes, until crisp. Turn off oven. Keep door closed and leave meringues in oven to dry. Cool completely.

Lemon Filling: Place egg yolks in the top of a double boiler and begin whisking them right away. Gradually add lemon juice and sugar; whisk until thick. Remove from heat and let cool. Stir in grated rind.

Whip cream in a chilled bowl until stiff. Fold lemon mixture into whipped cream. Spread lemon filling between the meringue layers.

Yield: 10 to 12 servings.

Notes: Can be made a day ahead, but keep the meringues and filling separate. Assemble shortly before serving time. Refrigerate any leftovers. Non-dairy whipping cream can be substituted.

Recipe by Myra Cohen

Neapolitan

A Neapolitan is a very popular tea dainty that can be made in advance.

Torte Layers:
1 egg
1 cup granulated sugar (scant)

1 cup ($\frac{1}{2}$ pound) unsalted
butter, melted and cooled
$2\frac{1}{2}$ cups all-purpose flour
pinch of baking soda

Preheat oven to 350°F. You need 9-inch or 10-inch round cake pans or 8-inch or 9-inch square pans. Greasing is not necessary.

In an electric mixer, beat egg; gradually add sugar and beat until creamy, about 2 minutes. Blend in melted butter. Sift together flour and baking soda. Add to egg mixture and mix just until flour disappears. Do not overmix.

Knead dough by hand for 1 minute. Divide dough into 4 equal portions. Pat each portion into a cake pan. (If you don't have enough pans, bake the torte layers in batches.)

Bake at 350°F for 15 to 20 minutes until golden brown. Remove from pans immediately and place on a level surface to cool. Fill and assemble as directed.

Filling:	¼ to ½ pound (½ to 1 cup)
2 packages (4-serving size	unsalted butter
each) chocolate pudding	1 cup icing sugar
(not instant)	toasted slivered almonds or
2 cups milk	crushed nuts, to garnish

In the top of a double boiler, gradually add milk into pudding, mixing well. Cook until thick. Cool slightly.

In an electric mixer, cream butter until light. Gradually add icing sugar; beat until well blended. Gradually add cooled chocolate pudding, mixing well.

Spread most of the filling between torte layers, ending with filling. Spread sides of torte with remaining filling. Garnish with toasted almonds.

Yield: 10 servings.

Notes: Chocolate filling may be made days ahead and stored in the refrigerator. Remove from refrigerator a few hours before using. Layers can be made several days ahead. Separate them with waxed paper and store until needed. After filling and decorating, it will take time for the layers to soften, so remember to prepare this dessert well in advance.

Recipe by Ronda Roth

Pavlova

Meringue Shell:	Filling:
4 egg whites	1 cup heavy whipping cream
1 cup fruit sugar (superfine)	(35%) (or 2 cups Cool Whip
2 teaspoons cornstarch	whipped topping)
1 teaspoon vinegar	2 cups peeled, sliced peaches
1 teaspoon vanilla	or nectarines and/or
	6 to 8 large strawberries (dip
	the tips in melted semi-sweet
	chocolate)
	toasted almonds, to garnish

Preheat oven to 300°F.

Meringue Shell: In an electric mixer, beat egg whites until soft peaks form. Gradually add sugar 1 tablespoon at a time and continue beating until stiff peaks are formed. Dissolve cornstarch in vinegar; add to meringue. Blend in vanilla.

Spoon the meringue onto parchment paper and form an 8-inch circle. Use the back of a spoon to shape the meringue into a pie shell, building up the sides about an inch higher than the center.

Bake at 300°F for 1 hour. Turn off oven. Keep door closed and leave meringue in oven to dry. Cool completely. Gently tip over and carefully remove parchment paper. Place meringue shell on a serving platter.

Filling: Whip cream in a chilled bowl until stiff. Fill meringue shell with whipped cream. Decorate with fruits of your choice. (If using peaches, add 1 teaspoon almond extract to the whipping cream.) Garnish with a sprinkling of toasted almonds. If using strawberries dip tips in melted chocolate. Put strawberries on toothpicks and stick them into sides of meringue shell.

Yield: 8 servings.

Recipe by Margaret Wayne

Sabayon Sauce

This sauce is rich and elegant.

8 egg yolks	1 cup sherry
⅛ teaspoon salt	2 teaspoons brandy
1 cup sugar	1 cup whipped cream
juice of ½ lemon	

In the top of a double boiler over simmering water, whisk egg yolks together with salt, sugar and lemon juice. Cook, whisking constantly, until thickened, frothy and doubled in volume. This will take about 5 to 7 minutes. Gradually add sherry and brandy. Remove from heat.

Let cool, whisking sabayon occasionally. (Place it over a bowl filled with ice water to speed up the cooling process.) Fold in whipped cream. Can be prepared up to 4 hours in advance, covered and refrigerated.

Yield: 10 to 12 servings.

Recipe by Anita Bender

When baking, follow directions.
When cooking, go by your own taste.
Laiko Bahrs

Fresh Strawberry or Raspberry Sauce

3 cup fresh strawberries (or 2 cup raspberries)	1 tablespoon sugar
2 tablespoons orange juice	1 tablespoon grated orange rind

Blend all ingredients together in a blender or processor until puréed. Pour into a small bowl, cover and chill thoroughly before serving.

Yield: about 1¼ cups.

Tip: Combine with fresh fruit and serve over angel food cake.

Recipe by G.G.

Life is uncertain. Eat dessert first.
Ernestine Ulmer

PIES, CRISPS AND FRUIT

Caribbean Apple Pie

Filling:
3 pounds (1.4 kg) medium to
large apples (Gala and
Yellow Delicious combined)
4 cups water mixed with 1
tablespoon salt

1 teaspoon flour
2 cups additional water
2½ cups turbinado (raw) sugar
¼ teaspoon ground cinnamon
4 tablespoons butter (or Earth
Balance buttery spread)

Wash and peel apples. Cut each one into 10 wedges and discard cores. Rinse apple wedges in salted water; drain well. Sprinkle lightly with flour.

Combine 2 cups water, sugar and cinnamon in a deep saucepan. Add apple wedges and rapidly bring to a boil. Reduce heat to medium and continue to boil until liquid has thickened slightly, forming a light syrup.

Add butter and cook just until melted. Remove from heat and reserve to fill unbaked pie crust. (If apple filling produces too much syrup, drain off most of syrup, reserving ¼ cup. Pour reserved syrup over drained apple wedges.)

Pastry for 2-crust pie:	**1 cup vegetable shortening**
3 cups all-purpose flour	**(Crisco)**
1½ teaspoons salt	**½ cup cold milk**

Sift together flour and salt. With a pastry blender or two knives, cut in shortening until mixture resembles coarse meal. Gradually add milk; mix rapidly with a fork, until flour is moistened. Knead lightly with hands, handling dough gently and quickly. Gather dough into a ball and cut it in half. Cover and refrigerate for at least ½ hour for easier handling.

Preheat oven to 380°F. Place dough on a lightly floured surface. With a floured rolling pin, roll out half of dough into a circle about an inch larger than a 10-inch pie plate. Cover dough with waxed paper and roll it up like a jelly roll. Place in ungreased pie plate and unroll carefully, being careful not to stretch dough. Remove waxed paper. Prick dough in several places.

Spoon filling into pie shell. Roll out remaining dough into a large circle. The thinner the dough, the flakier it will turn out. Place over apple filling. Press edges together with the tines of a fork and prick top crust in several places. If you like to be creative, cut out hearts or other shapes from the dough scraps and use them to decorate the top crust.

Bake at 380°F for 35 minutes, or until golden brown. Best when served warm, but wonderful cold the next day. For an elegant touch, top with sweetened whipped cream.

Yield: 8 servings.

Recipe by Gigi Martinez

Cranberry White Chocolate Tart

Pate Brisée:
2 cups all-purpose flour
pinch of salt
1 teaspoon sugar

1 cup (½ pound) cold unsalted
butter, cut into cubes
¼ to ⅓ cup cold water

Preheat oven to 425°F.

In a food processor fitted with the Steel Blade, blend flour, salt, sugar and butter until pea-sized clumps are formed. Do not overprocess. Add just enough water to form a dough. Cover and refrigerate at least 30 minutes.

Roll out dough to fit an ungreased 10-inch tart ring or a quiche pan with a removable bottom. To minimize shrinkage, refrigerate crust for 30 minutes.

Line crust with foil or parchment paper; weigh down with pie weights or dried beans. Bake at 425°F about 15 to 20 minutes, then lower temperature to 375°F.

Remove foil and pie weights and continue baking for 15 to 20 minutes until golden brown. (Keep checking to make sure crust is not getting too brown.) Set aside to cool.

Cranberry White Chocolate Filling:
2 cups (or more) fresh cranberries
³⁄₄ cup heavy whipping cream (35%)
12 ounces (340 grams) white chocolate, finely chopped
¹⁄₂ cup (¹⁄₄ pound) unsalted butter (at room temperature)

Put fresh cranberries in boiling water for one minute. Drain well. Transfer to a parchment-lined cookie sheet to dry and cool.

Place white chocolate in a large bowl. Heat cream until steaming hot (do not boil). Cool slightly, then pour over chocolate and stir until melted. Whisk in butter until combined.

Assembly: Line baked tart shell with cranberries. Spoon white chocolate mixture over cranberries while the chocolate mixture is still warm. Try to cover all the cranberries if you can. Chill for several hours or overnight, until set. Serve at room temperature.

Yield: 10 servings.

Recipe by Gloria Lepofsky

But I, when I undress me. Each night, upon my knees. Will ask the Lord to bless me. With apple-pie and cheese.
Eugene Field

Mayta's Apple Tart

1 cup sugar
1 cup all-purpose flour (do not sift)
4 tablespoons butter, cut in pieces

1 teaspoon baking powder
1 teaspoon vanilla
1 egg
4 large apples (or 5 to 6 McIntosh apples)

Preheat oven to 350°F. Butter a 9-inch or 10-inch springform pan.

Combine sugar, flour, butter, baking powder, vanilla and egg in a food processor fitted with the Steel Blade. Process 12 to 15 seconds, until the texture of cornmeal. Spread in prepared pan; press down to form a base.

Peel, quarter and seed the apples. Slice them in the food processor using medium pressure. Arrange in layers over base. Bake at 350°F for 45 minutes. While tart is baking, prepare topping.

Topping:
3 tablespoons sugar
3 tablespoons melted butter

1 teaspoon cinnamon
1 egg

Process the topping ingredients for 8 to 10 seconds, until mixed. Spoon topping over apple filling and bake 25 to 30 minutes longer, or until top is firm.

Yield: 10 servings.

Recipe by Mayta Markson

Peanut Butter Pie

Base:
1¼ cups chocolate wafer crumbs

¼ cup sugar
½ cup melted butter

Preheat oven to 325°F. Mix together ingredients for base and press into the bottom of a 10-inch spring form pan. Bake at 325°F for 10 minutes. Let cool.

Filling:
1 cup (½ pound/250 grams) cream cheese
1 cup creamy peanut butter
1 teaspoon vanilla extract

¾ cup sugar, divided use
2 eggs, separated
1 cup heavy whipping cream (35%)

Beat cream cheese, peanut butter and vanilla with half of the sugar until blended. Add egg yolks and blend well.

Beat egg whites with remaining sugar until stiff. Fold into cream cheese mixture.

Whip cream until stiff. Fold into cream cheese mixture. Pour over base, cover and freeze. Serve frozen.

Yield: 10 to 12 servings.

Recipe by Dr. Fay Weisberg

Pumpkin Chiffon Pie

Crust:
1 ½ cups graham cracker crumbs
½ teaspoon cinnamon
6 tablespoons butter
3 tablespoons brown sugar

Filling:
3 eggs, separated (reserve whites)
½ cup sugar
1 ¼ cups pumpkin purée
½ cup milk
½ teaspoon salt
½ teaspoon ginger
½ teaspoon cinnamon
1 tablespoon gelatin
¼ cup cold water
½ cup additional sugar

Preheat oven to 375°F. Lightly grease a 9-inch pie plate.

Crust: Combine ingredients for crust in food processor and process until blended, about 8 to 10 seconds. Press mixture into bottom and up the sides of pie plate. Bake at 375°F for 7 to 8 minutes, until golden.

Filling: Combine egg yolks with ½ cup sugar and pumpkin purée in a large bowl; beat well. Blend in milk, salt, ginger and cinnamon. Pour mixture into the top of a double boiler and cook until thick, stirring constantly, about 5 to 7 minutes.

Soften gelatin in cold water; stir to dissolve. Stir into hot pumpkin mixture. Let cool.

Beat reserved egg whites with ½ cup sugar until stiff. Fold into cooled filling. Pour filling into pie shell and refrigerate several hours or overnight.

Yield: 8 servings.

Recipe by Margaret Wayne

Strawberry or Raspberry Pie

Crust:
2 cups all-purpose flour,
  divided use
2 tablespoons butter

²/₃ cup vegetable shortening
  (e.g., Crisco)
¹/₂ cup orange juice
  concentrate, thawed

Preheat oven to 400°F. Crust: Reserve 1/3 cup flour in a small bowl. In a large bowl, combine remaining 1 2/3 cups flour, shortening and butter. Using a pastry blender, cut shortening into flour to form pea-size pieces. Make a well in the center and add orange juice; knead quickly. Form into a ball and divide to make two crusts.

Work with one piece of dough at a time. Flour the work surface and the top of the dough with some of the reserved flour. Gently roll out dough, pushing out from the center when rolling. Transfer dough to an ungreased 9-inch pie plate. Flute edges and prick bottom of dough slightly. Roll out the top crust; cover to prevent it from drying out while you prepare the filling.

Filling:
4 to 6 cups strawberries or
  raspberries
¹/₂ cup sugar
1 to 2 tablespoons lemon juice
1¹/₂ cups all-purpose flour

¹/₄ to ¹/₃ cup butter, melted
1 tablespoon brown sugar
¹/₂ teaspoon nutmeg
¹/₂ teaspoon cinnamon
pinch of salt

Rinse berries and drain thoroughly; pat dry. Place berries in prepared pie shell. Sprinkle with sugar and lemon juice. In a mixing bowl, combine flour, butter, brown sugar, nutmeg, cinnamon and salt. Mix well. Sprinkle over berries. Cover with top crust. Pinch edges of pie to seal well. Make several slits in the top crust so steam can escape. Place a pie catcher or aluminum foil on the bottom rack to catch drippings.

Bake at 400°F for 50 minutes, until golden brown.

Yield: 8 servings.   Recipe by Joanne Smith Cutler

Suzy Ballen's Apple Dessert

8 tart apples (preferably
Granny Smith), peeled, cored
and sliced
½ cup sugar
2 teaspoons freshly squeezed
lemon juice
½ teaspoon cinnamon
¼ teaspoon cloves
a few dashes of nutmeg

Topping:
¾ cup sifted all-purpose flour
½ cup sugar
⅛ teaspoon salt
6 tablespoons butter
½ cup walnuts, chopped
(optional)

Preheat oven to 425°F.

In a large bowl, combine apples, sugar, lemon juice, cinnamon, cloves and nutmeg. Mix well. Transfer apple mixture to a well-buttered baking dish or pie plate.

Topping: In a food processor, combine flour, sugar, salt and butter; process using several quick on/off turns, until crumbly. (Or combine ingredients in a bowl and cut together using two knives.). Stir in walnuts if desired.

Sprinkle topping over apples. Bake at 425°F for 45 minutes, or until apples are bubbly and topping is golden brown.

Yield: 8 servings.

Note: This is the finest apple crisp. It is absolutely delicious!

Recipe by G.G.

Cranberry-Orange Apple Crisp

Topping:
1/4 cup all-purpose flour
1/4 cup cornmeal
1/4 cup sugar
1/4 cup light brown sugar, packed
1/4 cup chilled butter, cut in small pieces

Filling:
7 cups peeled, diced Rome apples (3 pounds/1.4 kg)
1 cup fresh or frozen cranberries
2 tablespoons sugar
2 tablespoons grated orange zest
3 tablespoons orange juice
a touch of cloves, cinnamon and nutmeg

Preheat oven to 375°F. Spray an 8-inch square baking dish or 1 1/2 quart casserole with non-stick spray.

Topping: Combine flour, corn meal, sugar and brown sugar in a bowl. Cut in butter with a pastry blender or 2 knives until mixture is crumbly.

Filling: Combine apples, cranberries, sugar, zest, juice and spices in a large bowl and toss well.

Spoon the apple mixture into prepared pan. Sprinkle with crumb mixture. Bake at 375°F for 45 minutes, or until golden brown.

Yield: 9 servings.

Recipe by G.G.

Fruit Crisp

Filling:
6 to 7 cups assorted fruits
   (blueberries, cut-up plums,
   peaches or apples)
¼ to ⅓ cup sugar (or to taste)
1 tablespoon lemon juice
½ teaspoon vanilla extract

Topping:
½ cup (¼ pound) unsalted
   butter
1/3 cup sugar
½ cup all-purpose flour
pinch of cinnamon, nutmeg
   and ginger

Preheat oven to 350°F.

Filling: Put cut-up fruit or blueberries in a 9-inch deep pie dish, filling it almost to the top. Add sugar, lemon juice and vanilla; mix well.

Topping: Combine butter, sugar, flour and spices in a large bowl and mix until crumbly. Scatter mixture over top of fruit.

Bake at 350°F for 35 to 40 minutes. (If using apples, increase baking time to one hour.)

Broil the top until golden, being careful not to burn it. Serve warm or at room temperature with ice cream or yogurt.

Yield: 8 servings.

Recipe by Nicky Wernick

Rhubarb-Mango Crisp

Topping:
10 to 12 gingersnap cookies
¾ cup all-purpose flour
⅓ cup brown sugar, lightly
  packed
⅓ cup cold butter, cut into
  cubes

Filling:
¾ cup granulated sugar
2 tablespoons cornstarch

½ teaspoon cinnamon
¼ teaspoon nutmeg
¼ teaspoon ground cloves
2 large mangoes, peeled,
  cut into 1-inch pieces
  (about 3 cups)
6 cups fresh rhubarb, cut in
  ½-inch pieces (or 600 gram
  package frozen sliced
  rhubarb)

Preheat oven to 375°F.

Topping: Crush cookies into ¼-inch pieces. You should have about ¾ to 1 cup. In a medium bowl, place cookies along with flour and brown sugar. Stir well. Cut in butter with 2 knives until crumbly, about the size of peas.

Filling: In a large bowl, place sugar, cornstarch, cinnamon, nutmeg and cloves. Stir with a fork until well blended. Add mangoes and mix well. Rinse frozen rhubarb briefly, to melt ice crystals; pat dry. Toss rhubarb together with mango.

Then turn fruit mixture into an 8 or 9-inch square or round baking dish. Sprinkle cookie mixture over fruit, but do not press down. Place baking sheet under baking dish to catch spills.

Bake at 375°F on the middle rack for 45 to 50 minutes, until fruit is tender and topping is a deep golden brown. If necessary, cover top loosely with foil during the last 15 minutes to prevent over-browning.

Yield: 6 to 8 servings. This keeps well in the fridge for 2 days. Reheat in microwave or oven.

Recipe by G.G.

Baked Apples

4 to 5 apples (Northern Spy are excellent)
2 tablespoons pure maple syrup

2 tablespoons brown sugar
1½ cups apple juice
2 teaspoons melted butter

Preheat oven 350°F.

Cut tops off apples and remove cores. Make small slits around the top of each apple. Place in a large Pyrex dish.

In a small bowl, mix together brown sugar, maple syrup, apple juice and melted butter. Pour over apples.

Bake at 350°F until apples are tender, approximately 1½ hours, basting every 20 minutes.

Yield: 4 to 5 servings.

Recipe by Miriam Rubin

Curried Fruit

⅓ cup butter
¾ cup brown sugar, lightly
  packed
4 teaspoons curry powder
1 can (28 ounces/796 ml)
  pear halves, sliced

1 can (28 ounces/796 ml)
  peach slices
1 can (28 ounces/796 ml)
  whole apricots
5 maraschino cherries
1 can (8 ounces/250 ml)
  pineapple chunks

Preheat oven to 325°F.

Melt butter; stir in sugar and curry.

Drain fruit in a colander and pat dry. Place in a greased casserole or a low flat dish, which is more aesthetic. Sprinkle butter mixture over fruit.

Bake covered at 325°F for 1 hour, until bubbly and golden.

Yield: 10 servings.

Tip 1: Always make this a few days ahead. Reheat it at 325°F for ½ hour.

Tip 2: I usually double this recipe. It looks better aesthetically and it is still good days later.

Recipe by G.G

Pear Almond Gratin

¼ cup dry white wine	1 tablespoon grated lemon
1 tablespoon lemon juice	zest
1 tablespoon orange juice	½ teaspoon cinnamon
½ cup sugar	5 Bosc pears, peeled, cored
½ cup sliced almonds, divided	and sliced lengthwise
use	(½-inch thick)
1 tablespoon orange zest	

Preheat oven to 400°F. Grease 10-inch pie plate.

In a saucepan, combine wine, orange juice and lemon juice. Bring to a boil, then cook uncovered until liquid is reduced by half. Stir in sugar.

Chop ¼ cup almonds and mix with lemon zest, orange zest and cinnamon. Set aside.

Layer half of the pear slices in prepared pie plate. Top with chopped almond/zest mixture. Layer the rest of the pears and top with ¼ cup sliced almonds. Pour wine mixture over the pears.

Bake at 400°F about 25 minutes, until top is golden brown and fruit is bubbly.

Yield: 6 to 8 servings.

Recipe by G.G.

Pineapple and Raspberries

1 whole pineapple, peeled and
  cored
1 cup fresh raspberries

2 sprigs fresh mint
2 tablespoons brown sugar
juice of 2 limes

Cut pineapple into bite-size pieces. Place in a large serving bowl. Add raspberries, mint, brown sugar and lime juice. (A little tequila is good for festive occasions!) Serve chilled.

Yield: 6 servings.

Recipe by Richard J. Lewis

*Once in a young lifetime one
should be allowed to have
as much sweetness as one
can possibly want and hold.*
Judith Olney

Blueberry Flan

Dough:
1 cup all-purpose flour
½ teaspoon salt

2 tablespoons sugar
½ cup (¼ pound) butter
1 tablespoon white vinegar

Butter a 9-inch or 10-inch spring form pan or a 10-inch flan pan.

Combine flour, sugar and salt in food processor and process until mixed. Add butter and process for 10 to 12 seconds, until crumbly. Add vinegar and process just until dough gathers together and forms a ball, about 15 to 20 seconds.

Press dough into the bottom and one inch up the sides of prepared pan, flouring your hands for easier handling.

Filling:
5 cups blueberries
(fresh or frozen)

⅔ cup sugar
2 tablespoons flour
¼ teaspoon cinnamon

Preheat oven to 400°F. Wash and dry blueberries; reserve 2 cups for topping the baked flan. In a large bowl, combine remaining 3 cups blueberries with sugar, flour and cinnamon. Mix together and spread over dough.

Bake at 400°F for 50 to 60 minutes, until crust is golden brown and berries are bubbly. Remove from oven and top with reserved berries. Let cool. Delicious topped with ice cream.

Yield: 8 to 10 servings.

Recipe by Shaynka Farber

Index of Recipes

Index of recipes by contributor

NOTES

Cooking Kindness, Heroes in the Kitchen
A collection or recipe favourites

Please send me:

_____ copies of "Cooking Kindness, Heroes in the Kitchen"

Retail price $36.00 Canadian
All orders are in Canadian Funds $_____

Shipping & Handling (within Canada) to one address
$4.00 for 1 book plus $1.00 for each additional book $_____

Shipping & Handling to United States to one address
$10.00 for 1 book and $2.00 for each additional book $_____

7% GST (Canadian orders only) $_____

                                                   Total $_____

Ship to: (Please Print)

Name:_____

Daytime Shipping Address:_____

City: _____Province:_____Postal Code: _____

A gift from: _____Address: _____

_____

Payment by (please circle one)   Visa   Cheque

Card number:_____Expiration date:_____

Name of cardholder:_____Signature: _____

Please make cheques payable to: Gloria Guttman-Cooking Kindness

2300 Yonge Street, Box 2444,
Toronto, Ontario, Canada M4P 1E4
Tel: 416-440-7999, Toll Free 1-866-230-3269, Fax. 416-487-8932
Email: gguttman04@earthlink.net.

The net proceeds from Cooking Kindness are donated in support of the Israel Cancer
Research Fund.
Thank you for your support.